10-12-16(14)

PRAISES FOR

French Accents

"Anita's French style is both inspirational and aspirational. She has a distinctly personal—and approachable—way of combining the rustic with the refined. *French Accents* should be a go-to design resource for [adding] a bit of French style to your home."

—*Donna Talley, regional editor, producer and photo stylist,* Better Homes & Gardens

"I love how down-to-earth Anita is in her approach to French decorating, which so many women would like to emulate. With *French Accents*, she takes the idea of it being unattainable for normal folks with real budgets out of the picture and shares easy ways to add French touches in a fresh, simple, modern way."

—*Rhoda Vickers, lifestyle blogger, author of the* Southern Hospitality *blog*

"Anita Joyce has the most charming way to instill French accents into interiors. In *French Accents*, she shares her experiences, knowledge, and tips for incorporating the many iconic elements that define a French interior, [including] showcasing architectural details, . . . choosing a flattering color palate, uniting well-aged furnishings with elegant ones, or spot-lighting textures and finishes, to name a few.

"With an easy-to-follow plan, how-to list, and well-chosen examples, Anita takes you on a candid and informative step-by-step journey to achieve the much-loved look.

"Though your home might be far from the storied buildings of Paris, the cobblestone streets of the French countryside, or the lavender fields of Provence, *French Accents* gently demonstrates how to easily and effortlessly infuse character and right touches with confidence to any space, may it be in a farmhouse, a city home, a cottage, or a chateau.

"*French Accents* is a tribute to the essential and uncontrived mix of flair and function that epitomizes French style and *joie de vivre*."

—*Fifi O'Neill, author of several books (including* Prairie-Style Weddings: Rustic and Romantic Farm, Woodland, and Garden Celebrations*) and editor of* French Country Style *and* Tuscan Home *magazines.*

"The term *French decorating* used to somewhat intimidate me. Let's face it, when you yourself decorate with pallet wood, anything else sounds pretty upscale! Anita's approach changed all that. When I glanced through the pages of her inspiring book, one word came to mind: *Comfort.* You will find something in every single room you will fall in love with . . . no matter what you call your own style!

"Thanks for breaking that barrier down for me, Anita. I am a new French decorating fan!"

—*Donna Williams, founder of Funky Junk Interiors and author of the* Funky Junk *blog*

"Anita is a master when it comes to creating beautiful, livable French-style spaces. Yes, this book is overflowing with inspirational images to spark with your creativity. More than that, though, Anita's casual approach and friendly words make re-creating this style accessible."

—*Marian Parsons, founder of Mustard Seed Interiors and author of the* Miss Mustard Seed *blog*

"Opening Anita's beautiful book is like stepping into France at its ethereal best! Immediately struck by breathtaking Parisian images, you know you are in for a very special treat! The pages transport the reader into the fascinating world of French decor and old-world charm.

"Do not let the sublime images of French decor fool you. The book is down-to-earth practical and offers the reader an easy-to-follow system of getting an authentic French look. Anita spares no details as she takes us step by step from learning about French style to the finishing touches of several beautiful French-inspired rooms and do-it-yourself projects. *French Accents* is a storybook of one homemaker's love of all things French and her decorating journey as well as a savvy workbook to learn from and discover the art of French decorating.

"A true delight for Francophile decorators and the novice as well!"

—*Yvonne Pratt, author of the* StoneGable *blog.*

"I have been a fan of Anita's style and flair for French decorating for years. One of the incredible things about Anita is her ability to elevate even the most ordinary of things into something truly extraordinary with the true eye of a designer. She has inspired me and so many others with her creativity and photography and her beautiful French country decor. This incredible book captures the essence of Anita's style and grace and humor and inspires all of us to introduce a little something amazing in our own little corner of the world. Well done, my friend!"

—*KariAnne Wood, founder of Thistlewood Farms and author of the* Thistlewood Farms *blog*

FRENCH ACCENTS

FRENCH ACCENTS

FARMHOUSE FRENCH STYLE
FOR TODAY'S HOME

Anita Joyce

Plain Sight Publishing | An Imprint of Cedar Fort, Inc. | Springville, Utah

ISBN 13: 978-1-4621-1678-2

Published by Plain Sight Publishing, an imprint of Cedar Fort, Inc.
2373 W. 700 S., Springville, UT 84663
Distributed by Cedar Fort, Inc., www.cedarfort.com

LIBRARY OF CONGRESS CATALOGING-IN-PUBLICATION DATA
Joyce, Anita, 1961- author.
  French accents / Anita Joyce.
  pages cm
  ISBN 978-1-4621-1678-2 (alk. paper)
  1. Interior decoration. I. Title.

  NK2115.J77 2015
  747—dc23

  2015007613

Cover and page design by Lauren Error
Cover design © 2015 by Lyle Mortimer
Edited by Eileen Leavitt
Photography by Anita Joyce

Printed in China

10 9 8 7 6 5 4 3 2 1

Printed on acid free paper

To Kevin, for seeing me not as who I am but who I strive to be. To Elise, for showing me how to dance with the angels. And to Evie, for reminding me that life is an adventure.

CONTENTS

ACKNOWLEDGMENTS

I really want to thank my family for supporting me through the years with the blog and now this book. Thank you, Kevin, Evie, Elise, and Mom. Miss Haydee Cortez kept the home fires burning, while the two Evie's (Evie Joyce and Evie Sweeten) and Kelli Hays helped keep my blog running. I also want to thank Rit Johnson and Brandon Kinsey with Ridgewater Homes, Inc. for building my dream home. I appreciate the following people who were instrumental in the completion of this book: Bev Corte, Leslie Matula, Renee Diehl, Caroline Hayman, Becky Lanier, Cassie O'Reilly, and Cecile Johnson.

The reason I began blogging was because my friend Peggy Born believed in me. She read my blog, even when no one else did. Of course, none of this would have been possible without the Lord, through whom all blessings flow. I also want to thank my readers, who are generous and delightful. My blogger friends have also been supportive and gracious. I appreciate all of them, but feel I especially need to thank Yvonne Pratt, Debbie Peavy, Kim Nichols, Sharon Satoni, Donna Williams, Courtney Milton, Lisa Stauber, KariAnne Woods, Rhoda Vickers, Marian Parsons, and so many, many more.

Introduction

Long ago, during a difficult time in my life, I found myself mired in a pool of self-pity, wondering if there was more to life. Desperate for a diversion, I attended an antique auction on a whim, not knowing what to expect. The next thing I knew, I was on my way home with a handsome, tall French stranger. He—or more correctly *it*—was actually an eight-foot-tall antique French armoire. Still, I was in love! I could hardly contain my excitement as my eyes gently traced the intricate carving along the top of the piece. I marveled at the carved details, the arched door, handmade dovetail joints, and the age (over 150 years old). My mind wandered as I dreamed of who must have owned it and what their lives were like. Where did they live? Were their lives as romantic as I imagined?

I couldn't get the first French owners out of my head. More and more during the day, my thoughts turned to my armoire's previous life in France. I was drawn there in a magnetic way I couldn't explain. When I confided my growing obsession of all things French to my mother, she informed me of my French ancestry. I hadn't known about it before because the family name had been changed to an anglicized version over two hundred years earlier.

INTRODUCTION

Discovering my French roots not only legitimized my fascination with France but also made me even more determined to visit, even though I knew very little about France and spoke no French. In my mind's eye, I was there, basking in the sunshine amid a field of lavender, reading under the shade of a large gnarly tree or walking down a lovely boulevard in Paris to a nearby patisserie for a café au lait and croissant.

I convinced my husband to take a French vacation. Actually it wasn't that difficult to talk him into it. After a brief stay in Paris, we were off to the south of France. As we arrived in the Luberon Valley, I quickly declared it to be the most stunning place I had ever been. The little, dreamy town, high on a hill, looked much as it did hundreds of years before, with its cobbled streets and stone houses. Pots of gardenias lined the boulevard in front of the homes. In the distance, I could see laundry sparkling in the sun as it hung on the clotheslines. Each morning, I would throw open the old wooden shutters to reveal the glorious valley below.

As the sun's rays streamed in, it felt as if heaven itself had invaded the room. Birds sang in the distance, and I could hear the soft sounds of the village coming to life. Glasses clinked at the outdoor café nearby as the waiters prepared for breakfast. Neighbors greeted each other as they picked up their morning paper and opened their windows for the day. I loved everything about life here. People seemed happy; they enjoyed life, savored meals, and spent time outdoors.

INTRODUCTION

I remember thinking it must be the most glorious place on earth. Here I felt safe and isolated from the harsh outside world. I wanted to bottle it all up and take it home with me. And then a thought formed: *Why not?* Was it possible to live a French lifestyle back home? The seed was planted; the dream was born. I left home restless and unfocused; I returned with a passion and a mission. I wanted to live my life in the French way surrounded by beauty, savoring time with my family and friends. And so began the journey to teach my home to speak French.

This book is about the journey to create Farmhouse French style in a comfortable, inviting way that welcomes friends and family and makes them feel celebrated and loved. It includes DIY tips and tricks so you can do it all on a budget. This book is about adding Farmhouse French accents to your home—combining cozy, rustic charm with a quiet, elegant style.

CHAPTER 1: IS IT FRENCH?

Upon returning from my first trip to France, I found myself smitten with French decor. I was determined to convert my very plain, very seventies suburban American home into a country French retreat. There was only one catch—well, three to be exact.

1. I only had one French item in my entire home.

2. I was on a tight budget.

3. I had no clue what exactly constituted French design.

A sane person (or one with above-average intelligence) might have given up at that point, but not me. I was a woman on a mission. Telling me not to convert my home to French decor was like telling a fish not to swim. I knew it would happen, I just didn't know how I was going to get from point A to point B. I have found that a determination to do a certain thing is more important than the knowledge required to accomplish the thing. Sure, I didn't know what I was doing, but I wasn't going to let that get in my way. I looked at what I did know: I could look at a piece of furniture and tell if it was French or not.

I even found some inexpensive sources for French furniture; it was the rest of the stuff—the bedding, curtains, lamps, and accessories—that was the issue. How would I be able to look at a lamp, for example, and know if it was French or not? What about a candlestick? I started with what I knew was French—fleurs-de-lis, roosters, toile fabric, and of course the Eiffel Tower.

I decided that roosters would make my home look French. So I began to buy up every ceramic rooster within a fifty-mile radius. My house began to resemble a chicken farm, without the smell. In fact, one day a male friend was visiting and he asked if I had attended the University of South Carolina. I found the question very odd, and I asked why on earth he would ask such a question. "The roosters," he said. "Their mascot is a rooster. More precisely, they are the fighting gamecocks." Inside I was horrified that he didn't "get it," but on the outside I smiled as if he were the most clever guest we had ever entertained. Then, I began to wonder if my country French look was really working for me. (It wasn't.) I tried to reassure myself. I mean, really, he didn't know the first thing about design. I began to picture him living in a trailer park sitting in his underwear with a can of beer. Of course he was a nice man, but that day, I didn't like him very much. Couldn't he tell that is was first-class French design here? The nerve!

I began to rethink my whole "roosters + fleurs-de-lis + toile + mini Eiffel Towers = country French design." I realized it was time to do a bit more research. I decided I would work for a furniture and accessory store that specialized in country French decor. I worked there for about five years, spent every penny I made on furniture, and soaked up every bit of French design I could. I read magazines and books on French design. There weren't many decor blogs at the time, so I wasn't reading them . . . yet.

One day I found some new plates at a discount store. They were charming little salad plates in a soft blue, and they had a basket weave design. I thought they were charming and turned them over as I always do to see where they were made. "Made in France" said the stamp on the back. I hugged them and did a happy dance in the aisle. I had the real deal here. No matter what the plates looked like, they were French. Now I had real French dishes. And then I realized that if I hadn't turned them over, I would not have known they were made in France, so now I was even more confused about what constituted French decor.

So how can you tell if a basket, for example, is French or not French? What if it isn't made in France? Does it actually have to be made in France to give a room that French look? These were questions that I asked myself, and I began to form my own opinions on the subject. When looking at a country French room, it looked very similar to an English country room to me, with a few exceptions—more curves, flourishes, and extravagances.

I have not studied classic French design at a design school. The thoughts presented in this book are about how I created my own personal style I call *Farmhouse French*. Some elements of Farmhouse French style are not actually French at all but are simply things that appeal to me. I developed this style while chronicling the journey on my blog, CedarHillFarmhouse.com.

And here is what I have found: To create a Farmhouse French look in your home, you do not need to spend a fortune. You do not need to throw everything out that isn't French. You probably have many elements in your home that work with this design. If the item is consistent with

farmhouse or country French design and you like it, then keep it. French design is a broad category and has a lot of overlap with English and American design. If you are on a tight budget, you can do a bit at a time and gradually move your home in the Farmhouse French direction.

Common Myths

I think there are a lot of misconceptions about French design. Not only are people confused about what constitutes French design, but there are also some wrong ideas floating around that I would like to debunk.

Myth 1: French furniture is not affordable.

Obviously, some French furniture is very expensive. It has an eternal appeal, which means prices don't often go down. I have always said that if you put an English chair next to a comparable French chair, all other things being equal, the French one is usually going to cost more. However, French furniture can still be found for reasonable prices, and in some cases, it can be found for a bargain. When I was a kid, there was a popular saying: "It's all in the wrist." When young boys would be wowed by some super athlete and they would ask him how he did it, he would say, "Well, boys, it's all in the wrist." This would leave the boys with no clue how to do it for themselves, and it somehow made it sound even more elusive. For me, buying French furniture at bargain prices isn't in the wrist, but it is in knowing where to shop. The same chair, for example, might sell for one place at $150 and $1,500 at another.

Myth 2: You have to do an entire room in French style for it to look good.

There are lots of different French styles. On one end of the spectrum, there are those rooms that are quintessentially French, with layer upon layer of elegant and expensive French details, and on the other end, there are rooms with just one French chair. The

odd thing is that I've seen both work well. *French* is a style that transcends time. It works with many different styles, including contemporary, transitional, English, or country French. I'm sure there are exceptions to this rule, but I feel most rooms look better with French accents, even if the room itself isn't actually French. The other thing I have noticed is that French style is so distinctive that even if you just have a few French pieces in a room, visitors remember the room as being French. I remember when I first began collecting French furniture. I only had two French pieces in my entire house; they were two French armoires. Even then, friends referred to my style as French because what they remembered were the armoires.

Myth 3: French design is too formal for modern life

As with many myths, there is some truth in this one. Formal French design like what you might see at the Palace of Versailles is the height of formality and fussiness. Decorating a room as it would have been decorated for the eighteen-century French court is far too formal and impractical for today's living. But a French chair here and there, along with other French accents and touches, adds a bit of finesse to a room. On the other end of the spectrum, country French style (the style typically seen in country homes) has always been relaxed and easy. I think my farmhouse approach to French design is simple and fits well with modern life. I shy away from too much fluff and frills. I've worked to update my version of French design so it is cleaner and simpler. It just works better for today's casual lifestyle.

The bottom line is that you *can* do French design on a budget to fit your current lifestyle, without throwing out all of your current furniture. I would also like to add that it won't take you a lifetime to figure it out, because by the time you are done reading this book, you'll have several ideas on how to do it. Let's get started!

CHAPTER 2: START HERE

A beautiful room is not just a room filled with beautiful things. The beauty comes from how the individual pieces work together to create a room whose sum is equal to more than its parts. Consider this: the thing that makes a song melodious and memorable is not the specific notes that are used, but rather how the composer or songwriter weaves the words and the melody together. Sure, you need to use quality materials to make a beautiful room, but it is how everything works together than makes a beautiful room "sing." A sofa that feels harmonious in one room can feel like nails on a chalkboard in another, so you'll need to put some focus into studying how your pieces work together.

Good design means the room flows, has balance, draws you in, and says "stay." A beautiful room is one that comes together—a room that feels complete. It should feel cohesive and harmonious. It needs some symmetry but also some asymmetry. It needs varying heights and textures and fabrics that work together and don't fight. The most difficult part of interior decorating, in my opinion, is making it all work together. Since I am self-taught, when I work on a room, I am not thinking through steps taught in an interior design class. I am simply doing what comes naturally to me, without considering any formulas or design principles. It is like walking. I don't think about all that goes into walking from the car to the front door, it's just a part of life.

Having said that, I have made an attempt to document my process so I could share it with you. As I made an effort to think through how I approach a room, I realized I do have a process that I follow, more or less. I just wasn't aware of it until I sat down and thought about it. In this chapter, I'll outline the basic steps I go through, and in the "Before and After" chapter,

I'll walk you through how I transformed rooms at our farm, from start to finish.

I know, based on the emails I receive, that decorating does not come naturally to a lot of people. The focus here is on the "how to." It is one thing to pick out a beautiful chair, but making an entire room harmonious and beautiful is a different skill set. So where do you begin? At the beginning, of course! I like to start at my front door and walk into my house as a guest might on a home tour. I pretend it is the first time I have seen the house, and try to take everything in as a visitor would. I begin to notice things I had ignored before, like the dust bunnies in the corner and the dead plant.

I ask myself questions. Does the room feel warm and inviting? Do things flow? Are there places where one design stops abruptly and another starts?

I go through my house and make a note of everything that doesn't look right to me. If it is simply a matter of removing something, I can do that right away. If we are talking about replacing a kitchen table, then obviously I can't take the old one out until I have a replacement table.

Step 1: Take notes, listing the things you don't like about each room.

As you enter a room, take a fresh look at the room and try to see it with fresh eyes. Listed here are some questions to ask yourself about each room. Let these questions be a starting point. You can add your own, and take out the ones that don't make sense in your situation.

Step 2: Photograph the room.

Photographing the room helps you determine how your room looks in an unbiased way. There are problems that are difficult to see unless the room is photographed. Sometimes the room seems fine in person, but when you photograph it, you realize the wall color is too strong, or a chair is too big for the space. This is something DIY bloggers know. I thought the green walls in my daughter's bedroom were dated-looking, but I also thought they were still acceptable. I mean, they didn't look *that* bad. At least, that's what I told myself. When I took a photo to use on my blog, the photo told a different story. The room looked terrible to me! I might be able to lie to myself while walking in the room, but seeing it in a photo is another story.

QUESTIONS TO ASK YOURSELF

1. What is the first thing you notice about the room?

2. What feeling does it evoke?

3. Does it feel warm and inviting?

4. Is this a room you enjoy being in?

5. Does it feel dated?

6. What do you like about the room?

7. What would you like to change about the room?

8. Do you like the colors in the room?

9. Does the room feel cluttered?

10. Does the room flow or does it feel choppy?

11. Does it feel balanced?

12. Do the colors and patterns work together or feel like they are fighting?

13. Is the furniture functional for the room?

14. Is the furniture layout working for the room?

Step 3: Review decorating guidelines.

Read the chapter on decorating guidelines (see pages 25–42) and use those guidelines as you assess your room. They are generic, and are not specific to any particular style; however, they are important things to keep in mind. I chose to include these guidelines, even though they are generic, because I believe these guidelines will help you when decorating your home. Be sure to make notes as you go through the list.

Step 4: Review Farmhouse French list.

The Farmhouse French list gives you a list of specific things you can add to a room to give it a farmhouse feel with French accents. You don't need to incorporate all of the ideas, but these are easy ways to give your home a fresh Farmhouse French feel. Make notes on which items you plan to add to your room.

Step 5: Focus on one room at a time.

In general, I try to focus on one room at a time. For one reason, it's satisfying to complete a room, but it is not satisfying to have five rooms partially done. I like checking things off my list; I feel I have accomplished something. Another reason I like to take it room by room is that it is less stressful and easier to do. Keeping track of what is going on in one room is far easier than keeping track of three or four. Some days I can barely remember if I combed my hair, so my "one room at a time" approach makes my life more manageable. Working for a long time and not having one room actually finished can be demoralizing.

There are some exceptions to my approach. Sometimes you have a big project in a room, and no funds or time to work on it right away. I usually shelve those projects until my schedule opens up or I have the funds for the project.

START HERE

Another aspect of my strategy is to begin with either the easiest room or the one that is most important to me. But here is a tip: I keep the entire house wish list on my phone. I shop a lot at secondhand stores and consignment stores, and you bargain shoppers know how this works. Sometimes I see exactly what I want for a room, but that is not the room I am currently working on. If I really like it, and the price is really good, I go ahead and buy it, even if I am not officially working on that room yet. The item would be gone if I waited to make the purchase! Similarly, if I have painting projects lined up for several rooms, I often do them all at once. Painting is such a mess that I try to paint everything that needs painting, while the drop cloths, paintbrushes, and so forth are all out, and I still have my painting clothes on. Ditto on sewing. When I get my sewing machine out, I get on a roll and pop out the cushions, pillows, curtains, slipcovers, or whatever I am working on all at once.

Your decorating plan should include all proposed changes to the room. They might include

1. Furniture placement
2. Buying list
3. Electrical projects like changing a light fixture
4. Sewing projects
5. Upholstery work
6. Paint projects
7. Plumbing projects like a new sink or faucet
8. New flooring
9. Fabrics to be used
10. Furniture to be purchased
11. Tablecloths or other linens
12. Silverware
13. Dishes
14. Baskets
15. Artwork or Mirrors
16. Enamelware
17. Crates
18. Clocks
19. Lamps
20. Bedding
21. Accessories
22. Pillows and throws

Step 6: Develop a decorating plan.

This is one of the more difficult parts of decorating. It is often easy to see what is wrong with a room, but what should you do to fix it? The difficult part comes in deciding how to make the room shine. Sometimes the answer is as simple as rearranging the furniture, while other times, major pieces of furniture need to be replaced.

After you complete your decorating plan, you will have a list of things that you need to buy and a project list. Some things you might plan to buy right away, while other things may not get purchased for a few years. I try to not only make a note of what I want to purchase but also a time frame for purchasing, even if it just says *short-term* or *long-term purchase.*

Keep in mind some things probably won't work according to plan. Be flexible. The chair you bought for one room might look better in another. The rug you bought might need to be returned. Some things may not be returnable, so you will need to figure out what you will do if something doesn't work. That is another reason to have similar design for all of the rooms in your house. If something you bought doesn't work in one room, maybe it will work in another. Plan B is especially important when you shop at thrift stores, where returns aren't always accepted. Recently, I purchased a pair of chairs for my closet. The chair previously in the closet went to my bathroom, the chair in the bathroom went to my vanity, and the

stool at the vanity went to the guest room. If each room used different colors, then I would not have been able to easily shift the chairs to another room.

Step 7: Complete the decorating work.

Here you follow through with your decorating plan. Sometimes it can be completed in a day, while other times, if the work to be done is extensive and the budget is limited, it could take years. Don't stress if things in the room don't work. Just pull out what isn't working, and try something else.

Step 8: Review changes, and tweak as needed.

After you make changes to a room, take more photos and review them. Tweak the room as necessary. If you don't like something, or something doesn't seem quite right, try moving things around. Take things out, move things in from another room, or try exchanging the item that doesn't work. Remember, mistakes are okay and are part of the learning process. I tell my daughter all the time: everyone has failures. As one wise person said, "The only failure is one from which you learned nothing."

CHAPTER 3: DECORATING GUIDELINES

Even if you can't articulate your guidelines for decorating, I suspect you have some. It is like writing a sentence. There are millions of different sentences you can write, but still you need to be sure that your subject and verb agree. If you are a native English speaker, then you probably don't think about if your subject agrees with your verb when you speak; you just speak. You are not tempted to say "she walk" or "they walks." It's the same with decorating. There are many things that decorators may not think about that they just do automatically. For someone who speaks English as a second language, it's different. That person must then learn how to say things correctly and in a way that people can comprehend.

Before I started this book, I honestly never thought through what I was doing; I just did it. I experiment, I make mistakes, and I try new things. It can be a messy process, but I feel like the real proof is in the end result. In an effort to explain my design process, I made an effort to walk through it so I could capture it in words and share it with you—not unlike how you explain to a friend how to get to your house. You picture each turn and road in your mind's eye while you give the directions. That is how I captured a process I didn't realize I had.

Two Things You Need to Improve

If you feel that decorating doesn't come naturally to you, there is hope. I used to work with an instructional designer who told me something that rocked my world. She said that you can learn anything if you know just two things:

1. When you are doing "it" wrong.

2. How to fix "it."

I used these principles as a completely self-taught photographer. First, I first looked at my photos. The really bad ones got me excited because I knew I would learn the most from them. I would pore over each one. What was wrong with it? That list of what was wrong was long. They were often overexposed, underexposed, blurry, disjointed, boring, and so on. Then I would ask myself what I should have done differently. Those were the things I tried to change the next time. Most of the time, my corrections fixed the problem. But when they didn't, I kept trying new things until I was satisfied that the photo was done. It was a slow process, but by making every mistake possible, you learn a lot of wisdom that a teacher can't give you.

While it is true that some people are more talented than others, I believe with a bit of study and practice, we can all improve. This is why I recommend that you photograph your rooms. The photographs will tell you what is working and what isn't. Being able to identify what isn't working in your room is the first step. Sometimes you *know* what isn't working, but you don't want to know. The kind of things you don't want to know about include that large chair you just bought that is too big for your room, the pillow that is the wrong shade of blue, and the artwork that gives you the creeps every time you walk past it. These are just some of the decorating mistakes I have made along my decorating journey. It is because of the thousands of mistakes I have made that I feel qualified to talk about decor. I think I have made just about every mistake you can make, and I have learned from them all.

Guidelines

Decorating is about creating a home you love that loves you back. I am not going to tell you that you can't do this and you can't do that. I don't like rules. But guidelines are like highway signs, pointing you in the direction you want to go.

1. Avoid the fads.

I remember when ducks were popular in decorating (probably before your time). Everyone had ducks in their decor, or maybe it was just my mom. Then just as quickly as they came into fashion, they went out, and my mom was stuck with a house full of dated ducks. I'm not sure she even liked the creatures. So even if "everyone is doing it," *don't*, unless the look really appeals to you. Because when it goes "out" (and it will) you will be stuck with it. If it was a fad that is over, selling the stuff will be difficult. And really, do you want your house to look exactly like everyone else's house? I don't care if I miss a trend. If I don't like it, I'm *not* doing it. Now on the other hand, when I saw the trend of using grain sacks I jumped on that train, because I love them. They are historic. Many of mine date to the 1800s or earlier. They hold up well, and have a look that is difficult to replicate with new fabric. If the look goes out, I don't care; I'm keeping mine. That is what I mean about being selective about what fad or trend you follow.

DECORATING GUIDELINES

2. Don't be afraid to be different.

If you see a look you like, then try to re-create the look in your own home but with your own spin.

You have a unique style, so develop it! Find things you like, whether they are popular trends or not. If everyone is going blue and you like red, then go red! My grandmother loved red, and she had a red bedroom, even at a time when only brothels were red. She didn't care, and I applaud her for taking her own path. Don't worry about what everyone else is doing. The exception to this rule (excuse me, *guideline*) is when we are talking about the house itself and not the decor. Houses are expensive, and most of us are concerned about resale. So hold off on wild selections when picking flooring, tile, countertops, and any big-ticket items that will stay with the house. That way, the finishes will appeal to many buyers. As for your sofa, lamps, towels, and tables, buy what you love.

3. Don't go matchy-matchy.

I used to really like matchy-matchy everything. If I liked the chair, then I wanted the sofa, end table, coffee table, and settee to match it. I remember hearing that matchy-matchy was bad because then your house would look like a catalog photo for a furniture store. I thought, *What's wrong with that? I would* love *for my home to look as good as a catalog.* Then as I got older, I finally agreed with that sentiment. Catalog rooms look nice, but they don't look like someone lives there. They don't have a soul. I want a real home—one that looks like it evolved over time. I don't want a room that looks like I bought it all in one day at the same place. If things match too much, they can be boring and feel flat and fake.

4. Add the unexpected.

Maybe it's just the artist in me, but I like to have something unexpected and unique in my home. Usually I like to add at least one unusual item to each room. For my living room, I used an old iron fence post as the newel post on our stairway. I used empty frames on the wall in my dining room, and put sconces in the center of each one. In the bedroom, I hung my wedding dress and my mother-in-law's dress on the end of my armoire. I made our large walk-in closet a study. I remember reading about a designer who would hold dinner parties in his bathroom. I admit it sounded a bit odd to me at the time (I might be a bit of a germaphobe) but when I saw the bathroom (it was amazing), I thought, *Okay, I might be able to eat in here!* Now *that* is totally unexpected!

5. Think outside the box.

I wanted a Mora clock—a type of Swedish grandfather clock—and I mean I *really* wanted one. I saw them at the Round Top antiques fair for about $2,000 each. The price was for an antique clock that had been refurbished. I actually think that is a good price compared to some I have seen online, but I still couldn't justify paying that much for a clock. Instead, I looked for a repro-duction clock and found one. There was just one problem. It was black. It looked sturdy, and had a nice shape, but I really didn't like the color. The black color made it look contemporary, and I wanted it to look antique. So I bought it, tried out the black for about three days (that was as long as I could stand it) and then painted it gray. I love it now! So if you find something that you like, but it isn't quite right, think about if you could paint or change it to suit your own taste and style.

6. Create your own style.

I love the style of many decorators, but I don't try to copy them. For example, I love Charles Faudree's style. I adore it! He often used layer upon layer, and each room overflowed with French antiques. If I tried to copy his style, it would flop. At best I will only be a good imitator of Charles Faudree, but with my own style I shine; I am the expert. Be your own expert. Embrace your own style. Think about the mood you want to create. I used to think about whether I wanted a grand, impressive style or a cozy style. I decided that I wanted a home that embraced rather than impressed. Some of my style has evolved over time, but some of it—the warmth and the coziness—has been something I consciously chose to create. Think about the kind of home you want to create. Then choose pieces that support, or at least don't fight, with your long-term vision for your home.

7. Create a focal point.

A focal point is a point where your eye travels in a room. Each room has a focal point; sometimes it is what you want people to see, and other times it is not. This is where a guest's eye goes as he or she enters the room. Normally, this is the wall that a person first sees upon entering the room. So what I am saying is to put your best stuff there.

I want to wow people as soon as they walk into a room. If I had a "blow your mind" painting, I would want it to be the first thing you notice as you enter the room. Putting

Antique garden post converted into a stair newel post.

the best thing on the far wall as you enter the room isn't always possible because of the room layout. If that back wall is a wall of windows, then that is probably not the best place to hang your favorite painting or place your favorite armoire. However, you want that first glimpse of the room to be the best.

Think of arranging the room so that the first impression a person has of the room is the best it can be.

The artwork above a bed is often a focal point, and for the bedroom pictured on the next page, the mirror is the focal point. In fact, it would be difficult to not see it. The curvy French mirror on the wall draws your eye upward.

8. Don't line up furniture like soldiers.

We've all seen the expansive living room where the owners weren't sure what to do with the space, so they pushed everything against the walls. It ends up looking a bit like a cold, impersonal space. The chairs and sofa are so far apart from each other that you feel you

have shout to talk to each other. Be sure to put chairs close enough together that their occupants could have a pleasant conversation. If the room is large, you may be able to set up more than one conversation area in the room. It really is okay to move furniture so that it isn't all up against a wall. Our living room and kitchen are one big space, so it wouldn't have worked to push everything to the exterior walls. The kitchen is behind the sofa. I positioned the sofa and settees close enough together for conversation.

9. Let the light shine in.

Although heavy drapes certainly may be French, in today's modern home, most people really like light-flooded rooms. I know we sometimes need to close drapes, shutters, or blinds to protect fabrics when we aren't using the room, for privacy, or to keep the cold out. Still, when I am home, I like to have as much light streaming in as possible. That sunlight has a positive effect on my outlook and makes the whole room look cheery. If you do have old, heavy drapes on a window, I would consider removing them. Nothing dates a room like curtains that are past their prime. My mother-in-law must have believed that sunlight caused disease, or worse, disfigurement, because every window in her house remained shuttered all day long. Allowing the light to shine in makes the room feel much more happy.

> Furniture works best when put together as a seating arrangement close enough for comfortable conversation. The furniture doesn't always work when it is pushed up against the wall.

10. Hang artwork at the correct height.

You want to be able to see artwork without straining your neck. Make sure it is at eye level if you want your guests to truly appreciate it. Some homeowners hang their art too high on the wall. If paintings or photography are hung over a chest or a piece of furniture, then you want the artwork to feel connected to the furniture, so hang it eight inches or less above the furniture. A big gap between artwork and the console or chest below it makes the artwork appears disjointed from the furniture.

11. De-clutter.

Nothing ruins a room faster than clutter and too much stuff. We collectors are especially guilty of this one. If the room feels crowded, you won't like it, and neither will guests. If your room feels or looks crowded, the solution is easy and usually free. Remove something! Look around the room. What don't you like? What doesn't work in the room? Take those things out. If you like everything, then which items are your least favorite? If it is furniture and it doesn't work in another room, then give it away or consign it. The vanity shown here is a bit cluttered. Sometimes I get carried away. I prefer fewer items on the vanity. It gives your eye a place to rest. I know from my days developing statistic courses

Outdoor bistro chairs make for a cozy seating area to enjoy an afternoon cup of tea by the window.

that you need lots of white space on a page. Too much information on one page feels overwhelming. A room operates the same way. You want the eye to rest between the beautiful things in your room. Fewer items in a room can provide a soothing vista, while too many small things can create a feeling of stress.

12. Select paint color last.

I suggest you pick out your paint last, because the options are endless. Fabric choices (at least in patterns and colors I like) are very limited. It is much easier to find paint that works with your fabrics, than to find fabrics that go with your paint. Also, I suggest going with a more neutral paint color so if you change your color scheme later, you won't be forced to repaint each time. I've learned that lesson the hard way. That is why it is also good to use white on your ceiling, or at least a neutral color.

Another reason to choose your paint last is because you really need to see the fabrics and the other colors in the room with that room's lighting to determine the best paint shade. Lighting is tricky and different in every room. People often don't realize that different light sources can cause colors to look different. Being a photographer, I am very aware of the blue cast from daylight and a camera flash. Incandescent bulbs and a setting sun give off a golden light, while fluorescent lighting has a green cast. If the fabrics are in the room, then it is easier to check the paint color with the fabrics in the room's actual lighting. Be sure to look at the paint samples during the day and in the evening. A sample is easily applied to the wall or to a sample board so you can see how the color subtly changes

through the course of the day. Can't narrow your choices? Try several different samples at the same time.

13. Keep fabric patterns and number of colors to a minimum in each room.

I try to use no more than two or three prominent colors at most in a room. If there are too many colors, the room can feel confusing. It's also important to balance the colors in a room. One room of mine started out green. I changed the bedding to blue but still had some green accents on the other side of the room. In taking some photos of the room, I realized that one side of the room was blue and cream, while the other side of the room was mainly green and yellow. It wasn't until I saw the photos that I realized the two photos looked like they were taken in two different rooms. Had I not photographed the room, it would not have been so obvious that the room felt disjointed. When you work with neutrals, you don't have to worry so much about having too many patterns and colors in a room.

14. Add color with accent pieces.

Nothing says *cozy* and *come sit here* like a chair or sofa with pillows. Just be sure not to overdo it. This technique is also a great way to add an accent color or pattern to the room in small doses. Throws are another great way to add color or pattern to a room, and they can easily be cleaned or replaced when needed.

15. Use attractive decorative items for storage.

If you must keep certain items, like electronic remotes, in plain view, then organize them into a basket or box, so they look neat. If I have a choice of storing scraps of fabric in a plastic bin or an attractive wire basket, I am going to choose the wire basket every time.

16. Only buy things you love.

Only buy things you love. If you buy things just because they are the new trend or because they are the right color, you will soon tire of them. When you change color schemes or when the thing you bought goes out of style, you will no longer like it. But if you bought it because you loved it, you will want to keep it for the long haul. It's okay to have an eclectic style (a little bit of this and a little bit of that.) Sometimes eclectic rooms are full of things that are not really connected, but still they can work. One way to unify the room is to use just one or two colors in the room to tie it all together.

17. Add lights and darks.

My mother is a painter. She taught me about oil paintings, and I remember she said that you need lights and darks in each painting. It's interesting how an idea that works well in one visual medium works in others as well. When photographing, I try to have lights and darks in my photos, and I think a room needs both. We've all seen a room where everything is white. I *love* white, but I don't want every surface

Color can be added easily with pillows and throws.

Oyster baskets are a great way to corral things like towels.

in a room to be white. If you have a white table, then try using chairs that are not painted. If your walls are white, then go with a dark stain on your wood floors. Those are just a few of the ways to add lights and darks. Although I have painted a lot of furniture in my day, I don't want all of my furniture to be painted. I like seeing the stained wood. If you are using white furniture in the room, make sure you have at least one piece that isn't painted white.

18. Use similar color palettes in nearby rooms.

It is jarring to go from a room of pastels to a room of vivid colors. You want all of your rooms to feel like they complement each other. If you look at pictures from different rooms in your house, do they look like they all belong in the same house? You want things to flow from one room to another.

For a "decorator" look, try to give your rooms a similar feel. The colors don't have to be the same, but the rooms should feel like they were all designed by the same person. For example, if you love a French look, try to have something French in all of your rooms. If you love bold colors, then use bold colors throughout.

19. Don't fear mistakes.

Don't worry that you might make a mistake. I can tell you right now, you will! It will happen. But the good news is that you can

This dark console is paired beautifully with the light horse artwork.

learn from your mistakes. I learn more from my mistakes than I do from my successes. When I have a success, sometimes I don't know why it worked, so I am not sure how to replicate it. But when I make a mistake, I can usually tell you what I did wrong. And that means I probably won't make that mistake again.

As you can see on the next page, I changed out the bedding to the lovely mattress ticking set by Ballard Designs. I decided the artwork wasn't working with the new bedding. Then I envisioned a wall of ceiling tiles behind my bed. When they arrived, they were a bit stark white for my bedding, so I toned them down with a creamy paint. Still, the room felt a bit unfinished to me. I added a small mirror to the center of the tiles and a few blue touches. I didn't like that the pillows didn't match. The mirror on the wall was too dark and too small. I changed out the mirror for a larger silver one and added matching pillows. Then I removed the ceiling tiles altogether but kept the mirror and changed out the lamps.

The room evolved over time, and in the end I decided to go with what I loved—a French mirror. It was a bit narrow for this king-size bed, so I added some ironstone platters to either side of the mirror. Ironstone is something I also adore. In the end, I went with the French mirror and ironstone platters because they spoke to me. If you try something and it doesn't work, figure out what isn't working and experiment with different things. There is a lot going on here on the wall behind the bed. Because all of the colors here are similar (gray and white), the design seems to all work together in a calming way. If each plate were a different color or if there were several colors on the wall, I don't think I would like that much on the wall. I feel the ironstone was needed so the arrangement matched the width of the bed.

20. Shop your house.

Rather than running to the store when you need something, check your closets, attic, and other rooms in your home. This is a major blogger trick. If you want to give a room new life, first try moving things around from one room to another. I often get a fresh look by simply rotating things from one room to another. It is free and doesn't require you to leave the house. You can do this step in your pajamas. Sometimes a thing that didn't work in one spot will be perfect in another. If you don't move things around, you'll never know. If I can't find a home for something, it goes out the door to

Right: These photos show the various attempts at artwork and a focal point above the bed. In the end, I opted for something that spoke to me.

someone else. I shop my house all of the time. Remember the mirror that was too small and dark for that spot above my bed? I painted it with some gold metallic paint, then placed it on the little white side table in the same room. I think it added some oomph to the space. It's a good thing too, because that mirror was not returnable.

The mirror that was too dark and small above the bed just needed a touch of gold paint to work perfectly on this little table.

This old settee still has its original tapestry fabric, though it is threadbare in some places.

CHAPTER 4:
THE FARMHOUSE FRENCH LIST

There isn't really a formula to follow for creating a Farmhouse French room. I see so many beautiful French rooms, all unique and as individual as snowflakes. They are all so different—so one of a kind and lovely. What works for one owner in one room won't necessarily work for another owner or another room. I think suggesting that you should make your home fit some sort of mold would be doing you a disservice. I really do aim for you to showcase your interests, personality, and talents in your home. I don't want it to look like a cookie-cutter house. Your guests should walk into your home and feel at once that it is as unique as you are.

You can maintain your unique style and keep that Farmhouse French feeling—and here's the best part—without spending a fortune. The following are items I often suggest to my clients, both personal and professional. The items don't need to be made in France to work. That's the beauty of this list. I have baskets from craft stores that look amazingly expensive and French.

Here is my "go-to" list for things to create a Farmhouse French look:

1. Chairs

If you can't find a French chair, go with a curvy one. Often, it just needs a bit of flourish to add that feeling of elegance to

Right: This French chair was re-covered using vintage grain sack material.

Vintage wine crates sit below an antique French table.

a room. Many Italian chairs will work quite well. In fact, many of the crafts-men that made furniture for French royalty were Italian. Adding a French or French-ish (curvy) chair is by far the easiest way to add a French feeling to a room.

2. Side tables

French tables are a bit more difficult to come by, but certainly they are out there. Curvy furniture adds a French flair to a room. It may be difficult to tell if a box or basket is French, but it is usually quite easy to tell if a chair or table is French.

3. Mirrors

I feel like I am repeating myself, but curvy works, even if the mirror isn't officially French. The good news is that French mirrors are fairly easy to find. Mirrors are great additions to most rooms, so why not add one with lots of curves and personality? They reflect light and can make a room feel more spacious.

4. Chandeliers (wood or crystal)

A chandelier really does add elegance to a room. I hope you will use at least one in your home. We live in the South, where the heat can be oppressive in the summer, so we use a lot of ceiling fans. Where we don't need the fans, I try to use chandeliers as much as possible. We've used them in the kitchen, dining room, bathroom, closet, laundry room, and on the back porch. Be creative! And if you don't have electricity where you want to hang a chandelier, try using a nonelectric one that uses candles.

5. Rustic beamed ceiling

I know what you are thinking. If your house doesn't already have a beamed ceiling, you may think it is too late to add beams. Check with your carpenter. It may be cheaper and easier than you think. Decorative beams can often be added later. Crown molding might need to be removed, but that's not a difficult job for most professionals.

6. Baskets (especially rectangle-shaped baskets)

Baskets are incredibly easy to find. The difficulty lies in finding pretty ones that look antique or vintage. Look for vintage baskets at antique and resale shops. If you can't find good antique baskets, try looking for new baskets in gray tones. Square or rectangular baskets work great for stacking. Try stenciling numbers on rectangular baskets for a cool vintage look.

7. Wood accessories (bowls, trays, or totes)

Wood trays, bowls, and totes often evoke a country French feel. Antique or new, it doesn't matter; many of these items look great. I have an oversized antique trough that is quite beautiful. But even the small, inexpensive wood totes can add a bit of atmosphere.

THE FARMHOUSE FRENCH LIST

8. French script on anything

There are many items with French writing on them that are available these days, but you can also make your own. You can use stencils or other transfer techniques. My friend Karen, the Graphics Fairy (TheGraphicsFairy.com), has lots of free graphics and shares her techniques for adding the graphic to just about anything.

9. Silverware (bowls, pitchers, teapots, forks, spoons, trays)

Silverware is beautiful, and it adds bling to a room. The good news is that it tarnishes. Yes, that is the good news. Because it tarnishes, people get rid of their silverware by the truckloads. That means there are massive amounts of silver-plate things for sale. I'm talking about not only spoons,

Monogrammed grain sack on a
vintage ladder

Toile bedding with shutter doors
behind the bed

forks, and knives but also about trays, pitchers, teapots, and many more things. I don't mind a little bit of tarnish or even a piece missing some of its silvering; I feel that adds to the character of the piece.

10. Textured fabric like homespun linen, grain sacks, burlap, or drop cloth

Although traditional French fabrics often used cheery, bright colors like blue and yellow, neutral fabrics were still used for bedding and other purposes. Technically speaking, most of my grain sacks are not of French origin, but they lend the "farmhouse" feel to a room. My favorite fabrics to work with are linen and grain sacks, but sometimes I use burlap and drop cloth fabric. You can do amazing things with drop cloth. If you sew, you can use these fabrics for a variety of projects, but even if you don't sew, the grain sacks can be used as table runners or be filled with king-size pillows. When selecting premade curtains or bed linens, there are many linen options. Linen does tend to be more expensive, but it is worth it. I would rather have one set of good sheets than fifty so-so sets.

11. Traditional French fabrics like tapestry, ticking, and toile

What is French ticking? Ticking refers to a striped fabric typically used to make mattresses. It is often referred to as *French ticking* because this kind of fabric was used on many French mattresses. Now I often hear that term used to refer to any simple blue-and-white striped fabric. It is beautiful in its simplicity. There are several French ticking fabrics to choose from and products made with this type of fabric. Toile is a very traditional French fabric that usually shows bucolic scenes. There are many other beautiful French fabrics.

A white stoneware water pitcher with fresh flowers works well in almost any room.

12. White ironstone dishes

I prefer the old stuff made in England, but there are some beautiful new pieces available also. I don't think any of my ironstone is actually made in France, but it still gives a room an old feel, which reminds me of France and the French countryside. It is an important element of my style.

13. French dishes like Quimper

Quimper plates say *French* like few other things do. They are quintessential country French, but they are also difficult to find. They are usually colorful, so if you want to introduce color into a room, this might be a great way to go.

14. Chipped paint

If you love antiques, then it follows that you might like things with chipped paint. I love old things—things with history—especially if they have a worn finish. I love to imagine who owned them, how they were used, and all of the details of their lives. You can even antique new pieces to give them an old feel. Old furniture with chipped paint is a great way to add detail to a room. Antiques and vintage pieces are often one of a kind.

Now, let me clarify that when I was in Paris, I saw no furniture that was worn and chipped. There were furniture pieces in the high-end shops with lots of gilding but no chipped paint. The chipped paint is a great way to add farmhouse style to your home.

15. Something gold

Gold frames and gold mirrors are two examples of a way to bring in gilded wood. You can even paint something your-self if you like. Sometimes

Vintage stacking Florentine tables add a bit of Italian flourish to the room.

The rustic finish of these iron lamps works well with the reclaimed tin.

you can find a Florentine tray or table that is gold. Although the Florentine trays are technically Italian, I feel they work well with Farmhouse French style.

16. Ironwork

Rusty or non-rusty, beautiful ironwork is also something that has a French feel. Perhaps it is the porch railings I remember seeing in New Orleans, but ironwork does make me think of French design. You can incorporate iron into a room by adding something, well, iron. For example, you can add iron lamps, an iron door stop, or even iron stair railing. Sometimes you can find a bit of iron fencing to add somewhere.

17. Ruffles on pillows, bedding, or slipcovers

Ruffles are an understated way to add charm and softness to a room. They also help add feminine charm without using floral patterns. Ruffles can be used on furniture, slipcovers, cushions, and even pillows. Of course, ruffles work in other styles of decor, but they work especially well with French furniture because it often has a more feminine form.

THE FARMHOUSE FRENCH LIST

18. Painted furniture

Much of French furniture from the Louis XVI period was painted, so I tend to associate painted furniture with French design. I like having a few painted pieces in each room, but I prefer to have a mix rather than using all painted furniture. If everything is white, for example, it all begins to blend together. You need some contrast in a room.

19. Bottles and cloches

Old bottles and cloches give a room an old-world feel. If the glass is old, that is even better!

I have used everything on this list at one time or another. Farmhouse French style is subtle and requires a subtle approach. You don't need a room full of fleurs-de-lis or roosters or the Eiffel Tower to announce that a room is French. Let the room speak for itself—softly and elegantly.

Vintage and new cloches holding old books.

CHAPTER 5: WHERE TO SHOP

It is one thing to know what you need to buy. It is quite another task to find a place that sells it. It is difficult to find vintage items for your home in certain parts of the country, and it is also difficult to find reasonably priced French things. However, it can be done. There are many places you can shop online and locally. I cannot guarantee you will have great shops near your home, but there are lots of online options available to you.

Online Sources

I have bought from or worked with all of these online stores:

American Tin Ceilings
- tin behind bed at farm

Antique Farmhouse
- black porcelain hands

Anthropologie
- doggy robe hooks in master bath

Bali Blinds
- blinds throughout city house
- blinds throughout guest quarters
- city master bedroom drapes

Ballard Designs
- rug in city dining room
- rug in city living room
- curtains in city dining room
- wall decor behind city master bed
- candle sconce on wall of city master bedroom
- faux antlers above city living room fireplace
- chair cushions in guest quarters

Birch Lane
- rug in guest quarters

Blinds.com
- blinds in guest quarters

Online Sources continued

Decor Steals
- many of the white plates and platters in the city breakfast room plate rack
- bamboo rug in city study
- some of the white cake plates in city kitchen glass-front cabinets

Garnett Hill
- master bedroom linen sheets

Heritage Lace
- much of the lace shown, including the lace panels in the downstairs bath

Horchow
- city dining room chandelier

Home Goods
- most of the white dishes in the glass-front cabinets in the city kitchen
- chairs at farm dining table
- tufted chair in Evangeline's room

IKEA
- folding chairs at antique pine table on back porch

Joss and Main
- Reproduction Mora clock
- bench in city dining room
- wool blue ottoman in Evangeline's bedroom

Layla Grace
- white pillows on city master bed
- lavender print on canvas in city bathroom

Lighting Direct
- city kitchen island chandeliers
- city closet chandelier

NY Fashion Center Fabrics
- linen fabric used to make slipcovers in city living room

Pottery Barn
- bed skirt on guest quarters bed
- curtain rods in city master bedroom
- white bed covering in Elise's bedroom

Restoration Hardware
- city kitchen island French counter stools
- city dining room table
- city dining room console

Online Sources continued

Rustica Hardware
- hanging hardware for city barn doors to study

Soft Surroundings
- lamps in city dining room

Southern Honey Chawk Paint
- used extensively, many of the pieces were painted with this paint including the Mora clock, the French cupboard in the city dining room, and the iron bed in the guest quarters

Target
- bottle lamp in guest quarters
- large green bottle in guest quarters

Thermador
- 48-inch gas range in city house kitchen

Turkish T
- towels and lavender robes by the city master pedestal tub
- pink throws at the foot of the beds in girls' farm bedroom
- blue striped towel in downstairs bath
- white tablecloth used on city dining room table
- tablecloth at farm, on back porch pine table

Vintage Tub and Bath
- pedestal tub in the city master bath
- claw-foot tub in the downstairs bath

Wisteria
- column table by bed in guest quarters
- sofa table in city living room
- round farm dining table

World Market
- chair at vanity in city master bedroom
- backless bar stools in kitchen
- furniture at treehouse

Local Sources

Although I enjoy the convenience of shopping online, I also love going into local stores, where you can touch and see the merchandise in person. In high-end boutiques, antique shops, and thrift shops, you can sit in a chair, touch the fabric, and see for yourself the difference between a Louis XV and a Louis XVI chair. Here you learn. You can ask the shopkeeper why one piece is more expensive than another. The owners are usually quite knowledgeable. I shop a lot at resale shops, but also love to go into high-end boutiques. There I get ideas and sometimes make purchases. Don't be embarrassed to ask if there are any sales going on. Trust me, you won't be the only one asking.

Round Top Antique Show

Round Top Antique Week is one of my favorite times of

Here's a list of stores that I love to visit in person:

- *A&G antique mall* (facebook.com/AGAntiquesonnWest19th)
- *Alabama Consignment* (alabamafurniture.com/home.php)
- *August Antiques* (bensantiquegardening.com/augusta.html)
- *Chippendale Antique Mall* (chippendaleon19th.com)
- *Heights Antiques on Yale* (facebook.com/pages/Heights-Antiques-on-Yale-LLC/132424207920?fref=ts)
- *High Fashion Home* (highfashionhome.com)
- *Jubilee* (jubileeshop.com)
- *Laurie's Home Furnishings* in Tomball (laurieshomefurnishings.com/)
- *Leftovers* (leftoversantiques.net)
- *Rachel Ashwell Shabby Chic Couture Shop* (theprairiebyrachelashwell.com/shop.html)
- *Stillgoode* (stillgoode.com)
- *The Antique Gypsy* (theantiquegypsy.com)
- *The Pomegranate* (funkyartcafe.com/ordereze/Content/3/Summary.aspx)
- *Three Doors* (threedoorshouston.com)

the year. The shows happen once in the spring and once in the fall. The antiques and junk stretch for miles and miles along the Texas Highway 237 and beyond. Visit the website at AntiqueWeekend.com for details. You will think you died and went to junk heaven. I get a lot of my goodies here.

Fresh flowers by the bed makes for a great start to the day.

One of my favorite venues at Round Top is Marburger Farms (roundtop-marburger.com). I usually want one of just about everything they have there.

Another favorite of mine is The Big Red Barn (roundtop-texasantiques.com).

But you can't go wrong if you just stay on Highway 237. It is such a feast just taking in all of the sights and sounds. The food is much better than you would expect too. There are venues in other locations as well. Just be sure to check the maps for locations and dates.

Visit the website to see the schedule, map, and everything else you might want to know.

Yard sales

Yard sales are a great place to get a good deal. The downside is they require lots of driving around, and they are a mixed bag. Some will have a lot of what you are looking for, but most won't. If you are on a strict budget and have the time to go, I think they can be fun, and on occasion, you will discover a "pot of gold" find. I found that often it was disappointing to have spent my entire morning driving around only to find the kind of stuff that I too was trying to get rid of. If you do go, be sure to go early in the day on the first day of the sale. Most yard sales are pretty picked over if you arrive on the second day or even late on the first day.

Auctions

I personally adore attending auctions. Not only do they usually have some good stuff for a decent price, but the bidding is so much fun. Who thought up this method of selling stuff anyway? That person must be the most talented salesman ever. To refer to buying something as *winning* is brilliant. When the gavel goes down, and my buyer number is called out, I admit it's quite exhilarating, especially if there has been a bidding war. Of course when you win it, that means you agreed to buy it for more than anyone else in the room was willing to pay for it. But the bid amount is not what you actually pay for your item. You have to tack on the buyer's premium (a percentage that each auction house adds to your bill) and the tax. If the item is too large for your vehicle, there will be a delivery fee as well.

These rustic pencils by the bed mean you can write down that fabulous dream from last night.

There are two types of errors you can make at the auction:

1. You can get caught up in the excitement and end up paying much more than you intended.

2. You can be so conservative that you miss out on a one-of-a-kind piece because the price went slightly over a limit you had set.

So you could end up paying too much for something or miss out on the opportunity to buy something rare and unique. You have only seconds to decide before the gavel goes down. Most of the time, I let something get away, and I regret not bidding just a bit more for it. As I have said before, as long as you can afford it, buy what you like and walk away from a bargain that is just so-so.

Here are my auction tips:

1. Find an auction house near you.

Try websites like Auctionzip.com to find auction houses in your zip code or nearby. I wouldn't bother asking antique stores. Often antique stores buy their merchandise there, so they are not going to divulge their source. Antique sources are often guarded closely. We used to purchase antiques from a nearby antique store that carried beautiful antiques. One day, my husband asked where she got her antiques and she gazed into the distance, with a wistful look, and described fanciful, romantic trips to France to select and purchase her furniture. We were mesmerized. It sounded so exotic and exciting! Years later, I ran into the shop owner at a local auction. Then every time I went, she was there. Her secret was out!

2. Preview online.

A lot of auction houses have websites, and typically you can preview the auction online. This is a marvelous service, and it can save you a lot of time. I still recommend that you inspect the item thoroughly before bidding. The purpose of the online preview is not to inspect the item, but to determine if the auction is worth your time to attend. If you don't see anything you like, stay home and do something else. If you find something you can't live without, you can still check it out thoroughly before the auction. You can continue to preview items during the bidding, but it's a bit more difficult. You risk the auctioneer taking bids on an item you didn't look over yet. You can often bid online and over the phone. If you decide to bid remotely, be sure to call the auction house and ask for a condition report on the piece, because you won't be able to inspect it in person.

This gorgeous lamp looks right at home in front of a French mirror.

3. Know the going price.

Bidding is fun, and it is easy to get caught up in the thrill of the moment. With your adrenaline rushing, you might agree to pay a ridiculous price for an old pair of shoes. Auction prices are usually close to wholesale, but that isn't always true. The more people who are in attendance, the higher the prices are going to be. And if the auction house offers online and phone bidding, you could be bidding against any number of people not in attendance. Make sure to do your homework ahead of time. Know what the item is worth before you bid, and more important, know what the item is worth to you. If you know that type of chair or dresser is often available at the antique mall or auction, then I would not be willing to pay over what I know the going price is for that item. If, however, the item is extremely rare and I really, really want it, I would be willing to pay much more. Sometimes the item is so unusual that you can't find it in any store.

Just keep in mind that sometimes bidding gets out of hand, and the price can quickly skyrocket. Know what you can buy the item for in a store. Knowledge is power. If bidding gets out of hand, be prepared to walk away.

4. Know the buyers' premium.

Most auction houses have a buyers' premium. This is a commission, for lack of a better word, that you pay the auction house on top of the bid amount. The auction that I attend most has a buyer's premium of 15 percent, while another one has a buyers' premium of 20 percent. They seem to keep going up. Be sure to add in the buyers' premium to the amount you are bidding. If a chest would sell for $500 at a store, but you can get it for $400 at the auction, is that worth the hassle of attending the auction and having to go on their schedule rather than shopping at your leisure? Let's say you had a winning bid of $400, and then the buyer's premium is 20 percent. Twenty percent of $400 is $80, meaning the actual price you are paying is $480, plus tax. So you actually only saved $20, plus the tax on the $20. Considering that the auction house is a drive for me, and I have to go at a time of day that often doesn't work for me, a $20 savings is not worth it. More and more you can bid online and by phone, so that is an option for you to consider.

5. Look over the item closely before bidding.

I preview online to see what items will be in the auction, and I do a close inspection before the auction to ensure there is no hidden damage or defects. Don't be afraid to walk around the room during the auction. It is better to be safe than sorry, because once you win the bid, it's yours with no returns. If there is an obvious problem with the piece, the auctioneer may point it out, but subtle problems are not often mentioned because it is your responsibility to check the item over carefully. Buyer beware, so be safe or be sorry. If you want to bid online or by phone, call the auction house and ask for a condition report on the item.

A stone bird next to a little house-shaped shelf adds charm to the porch.

6. Don't wave at your friend during the auction.

It is just best not to move your arms about during an auction unless you are actually bidding. The auctioneer is a master of knowing who is bidding and who isn't, but he or she still isn't a mind reader. If you must move your arm, or scratch your nose, avoid eye contact with the auctioneer, while doing so. He or she will probably know you are not bidding. If you are looking at the auctioneer, don't nod your head or move your arm about. I have seen that interpreted as a bid, and it can be confusing to the auctioneer. I just think it is more polite to not make the auctioneer work so hard; don't make them guess. Some auction houses may be less forgiving and expect you to pay up on accidental bidding. One time, a friend who was actively bidding on something nodded her head in response to my question, and the auctioneer took it as a bid.

7. Set a maximum bid.

Before I start bidding, I have a figure in my mind of what I think the item should go for and what I am willing to pay. I make sure to factor in the buyer's premium also. Once the bidding reaches my maximum, I stop. Period. I have a fear that I will be caught up in the excitement and go crazy, so I limit myself. It's probably a good thing.

8. Know what will fit in your vehicle.

It is not unusual for me to end up with a large piece of furniture in my car. It happens more than I care to admit. I know what will fit and what won't. It's like a sixth sense, honed over many years of furniture buying. You will want to know if what you are buying will fit. If it won't fit, then you will need to consider the cost of delivery and roll that into the price. Most auction houses do not deliver, but they can usually recommend a good delivery service.

9. Don't be intimidated.

I used to look around the room and assume everyone there was much more knowledgeable than I was about antiques. At some point, I realized that most of the people attending the auctions are not experts. Many have some knowledge, but very few are actual experts. They are buying what they think they can sell in their shop or for personal use. Sometimes I see items at the auction that are clearly reproductions. The auction houses often include consignment or estate pieces in with the regular antique auctions, so being able to tell the age of a piece is helpful. If you are unsure and want to know, ask someone who works at the auction house. They are usually happy to give you their opinion. If you want to determine the age of a dresser or chest, one of the best places to look is inside drawers and on the back. If it looks pristine and uniform, it is NOT an antique. Also check the dovetail joints. Are they uniform or nonuniform? If the dovetail joints are all exactly the same size, then the piece was machine made, making it newer. If the joints are all different sizes or shapes, then it was probably handmade, placing it much earlier. Chairs can be examined from the bottom. The more you look at antiques, the more you will begin to know the antiques from the reproductions. You will get a feel for how something really old looks.

If you want to know what old stuff looks like, spend some time hanging out at an antique shop. Ask questions and examine the furniture. You can learn a lot from that experience. If the shop owner was helpful, try to buy something there. He or she just gave you a valuable, free lesson.

10. Have fun.

I enjoy going to auctions. It is something fun for me to do. Sadly, I don't have as much time to attend and I have less and less need to attend for my own house. However, it really is an adventure, and I encourage you to go at least once. The people-watching opportunity alone makes it worth the trip. There is usually at least one dog in attendance dressed in a snazzy outfit. I'm not sure why that is. Some auction houses attract buyers who are wearing high heels, dressed to the nines, and carrying Yves Saint Laurent bags, while others appear to bring in a rather sketchy crowd. Either way, I always have fun.

Craigslist

Here are my tips for buying on Craigslist, including a few safety tips to keep in mind:

1. Call, don't email.

If there's a phone number in the ad, then call, don't email. Callers are often given priority over emailers. And since many of the emailers are spammers, some sellers only respond to callers.

2. Contact the seller immediately.

If it is a fabulous piece, it will typically only be available for a few hours. I had a seller say he was holding an item for me, but that turned out to not be the case. Don't count on the seller holding it for you, even if he or she says he will. The safest bet is to purchase and pick it up as soon as you can.

3. Ask for a phone number.

If the ad did not have a phone number, be sure to ask for one. You may get lost and need directions, or you may need to cancel at the last minute.

Silver is an easy way to add bling to a room.

4. Confirm your appointment.

You don't want the seller to forget you are coming. And if the item is sold, you want to know before you leave the house, so be sure to verify your appointment.

5. Bring cash.

Because many sellers won't accept checks, especially on big-ticket items, it is always best to have cash with you. Bring smaller bills in case the seller will accept less.

6. Check out the item thoroughly.

Be sure to check the bottom, back, and sides. Look for damage and wear and tear. Make sure it is in acceptable condition. You will probably not be able to return it if you notice something later.

7. Leave your fancy car at home.

If you show up in an expensive car, don't expect the best price. Showing up in Mercedes will not make the seller sympathetic to your budgetary issues. I don't recommend haggling to get a better price if you show up wearing Gucci either.

8. Ask for the best price.

There is probably some negotiating room. I usually ask, and when I ask, I have always been offered a lower price. I don't ask for a better price if the asking price is already super low or if I can see the person needs the money. I also try to be polite when I ask.

9. Don't point out all of the flaws.

Showing the seller what is wrong with the piece is not a good strategy to get a better price. Having worked in a furniture store, I can't tell you how annoying this is. Just ask if the price is the best one, or if there is negotiating room on the price. The owner is probably aware of the defect and has already adjusted the price accordingly. A buyer that is nice will be given a better price than a buyer that comes off as critical.

10. Go with a friend.

If you feel uncomfortable going alone, ask a friend to go with you. If you can't find anyone to go with you, you can tell a friend when and where you will be and ask him or her to call you at a certain time. If you don't answer, that person will know where to send reinforcements.

11. Meet in a public place.

I have met people at their homes, but trust your intuition and never take chances if you have an uneasy feeling about a location or a seller. When possible, it is safest to meet in a public location. If it is a piece of furniture, this may be difficult to arrange with the seller. Use your best judgment.

Antique Stores

I used to avoid antique stores because they seemed to be the most expensive places to buy from, but recently I have found some great deals at antique stores. Just keep location in mind. Fancy addresses have fancy prices, and valet parking at the antique store is a good sign that you'll be paying more than you ought to. Less fashionable parts of town have better prices. Antique malls can also be nice places to shop. Just do your homework, so you can compare prices. The more educated you are, the better you will know your options and what is a good price.

Resale or Thrift Stores

Thrift or resale shops are usually linked to a charity. They are stocked with items that were donated to them. The thrift stores that accept consignment items are the best ones. Because people don't often donate their nice things, the shops that handle consignment items have a better selection and nicer things but still have wonderful prices. Often finding the best places to buy requires some research.

Consignment Stores

Not all consignment stores are equal. Some have high-end items, while others feel more like a garage sale. The stock at a specific store can also vary from week to week. Definitely take a look in your area to see if you have any nearby. They are usually priced a bit higher than thrift stores, but they tend to have nicer items. The other thing to keep in mind is that the price often goes down the longer the item has been there. Be sure to ask about their markdown policy.

eBay

A great place to find things is eBay—with a few caveats. Antique furniture seems ridiculously overpriced. With the price of fuel, it often doesn't make sense to buy furniture on eBay if you then have to pay for shipping. I do not buy furniture on eBay, but I do buy a lot of other things on eBay. I recently wanted a toast rack. Have you ever looked for a toast rack? They are not easy to find. I didn't want to drive all over town looking for one and likely come home empty-handed. I am careful about not buying anything too heavy on eBay because of the shipping cost. And if the item is not in the US, beware! I did this once, and after the sale, the seller pressured me to pay an additional fee for faster shipping. I paid the fee and ended up paying a ridiculous sum for a Fortnum and Mason basket shipped from Great Britain. Now I only buy small, lightweight items on eBay that are located in the US. Here is a list of things to consider when buying on eBay:

1. Know the shipping cost.

Make sure you know ahead of time what the shipping cost will be. It is usually listed, but if it isn't, send the seller a question requesting a shipping quote. Some sellers only charge for actual shipping costs, while others charge a handling fee. Sometimes the handling fees are too high. Make sure you know the total cost of shipping and handling before bidding.

2. Know the market value.

Having an idea ahead of time what the item should sell for is helpful. If you don't know what the item would sell for in a store, then you won't know if you are overpaying.

3. Set your price limit.

Know the top price you are willing to pay ahead of time and stick with it. This way you won't get caught up in the excitement of bidding.

4. Check seller feedback.

Verify that the seller has lots of feedback, and that it is at least 98 percent positive. I look for thousands of reviews, not just a handful.

Hang a chandelier on a bird cage stand for instant glamour.

5. Know where the seller is located.

Know where the seller is shipping the item from, since you will be paying for that shipping. Is the seller in another country? Would you be able to reach him or her if you had an issue? Is the shipping cost going to be worth it? Personally, I have made the decision not to buy outside of the US.

6. Buyer beware.

Read the description carefully and assume nothing. Often you can't return these items. Even if you can, you will likely be responsible for the cost of return shipping, and you will have the hassle of returning the item.

7. Ask questions.

Think of everything you might want to know before purchasing the item. If the description does not answer all of your questions, don't hesitate to send the seller any unanswered questions. Do this before bidding.

8. Verify smoke-free condition.

Make sure it is from a smoke-free home, unless a smoke smell isn't an issue for you. Many, if not most of the items on eBay are from smoke-free homes, but still I would check. If the seller has lots of positive feedback, you are probably safe. If you don't ask, and it doesn't specify, you may not be able to return it for smoke odor. Be safe and verify. Often it clearly states that in the description.

9. Verify pet-free condition.

Often, items are from a pet-free environment, but not always. If you are allergic, make sure the item has not been exposed. Returns are no fun for anyone, and sometimes they are not accepted. Again if it doesn't specify, be sure to ask.

10. Know the shipping policy.

The bigger sellers have a shipping policy, meaning they state how often they ship. So if they ship on Saturdays and you purchased on Tuesday, you can expect your item to ship the next Saturday. Delivery dates will vary depending on how far you are from the shipping location. They will often state who the carrier is and if tracking information will be provided. Be sure you understand how they operate before you bid. You don't want to be waiting a month for something you thought would arrive in a few days.

11. Know if insurance is included.

Some sellers will include insurance in their shipping fees, while others do not. Be sure you know what you are paying for. If you do want insurance and it is not included, simply ask if you can add it. Conversely, if they include insurance and you don't want it, you can always ask for that fee to be removed.

12. Pay promptly.

It's just common courtesy to pay for an item as soon as you win the bid. I try to pay immediately. Don't leave the seller wondering if you will make good on your purchase. And if you need more incentive, they are rating you as a buyer. You want lots of positive feedback that other eBayers will see, whether you are buying or selling. Some sellers will only do business with buyers who have met a minimum rating.

13. Leave feedback.

After receiving the item, leave feedback for the seller. The feedback is extremely important. This is how the seller proves he or she is reputable, so your rating is important. If you had a bad experience, try to resolve it with the seller before you leave bad feedback. Bad feedback really hurts sellers. The reputable ones will usually go out of their way to make you happy. But if you don't tell them, they can't fix it.

CHAPTER 6: FOUND OBJECTS & COLLECTING

Found Objects

Want to add instant charm to your room? If you want your home to feel warm, unique, and magazine worthy, one of the best ways is to include vintage or antique pieces in your home. Vintage items are an important element in Farmhouse French style. I'm amazed what a difference they make in a room. Old things are so fascinating to me. Sometimes I feel like they should be in a museum, but instead, I get to hold and touch them. I have an original Louis Felippe mirror from pre-1850 France. I have a few other pieces from the nineteenth century as well. I wonder who that mirror saw before me.

Antique items are defined as things over one hundred years old. Vintage refers to items over twenty years old, but not quite one hundred years old. I'm going to be discussing them together as one group of things. They are, in a word, old. Old things are different than new things. I like to see a mix of old and new in a room. The new things give the room life, and the old things give it character. A room full of only new things seems off to me. It's difficult to explain; a room with only new things seems to lack soul. I want to see something unusual, something I can't just go to the mall and buy.

For example, what kind of new table would have the character that these tables do?

Using hanging hardware for doors instead of traditional
hinges adds farmhouse style to a room.

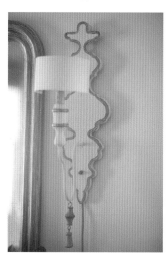

Or what about these doors? Would a regular new door give the room this much personality?

These vintage wall sconces add texture and a bit of drama. Vintage ceiling tiles are also a great way to add instant vintage style to a wall.

You can use vintage or antique materials when building your home. We added antique corbels and salvaged boards to make a shelf in our hall.

Right: A shelf like this could be added
to just about any home.

Old iron pieces like these shown are not only attractive, but they also provide extra storage space.

Salvaged beadboard made for a unique one-of-a-kind porch ceiling.

Clocks

Many old clocks are beautiful works of art. I don't actually use them to tell time, but you could. They add a beautiful, historical feel to the room.

Seltzer bottles

Seltzer bottles are increasing in popularity, and they look great when displayed in a bar area or when collected and displayed together.

Statues

Statues are often very elegant. They add an element of three-dimensional art in a room. I love to stare at them, wondering who posed for the artist and what his or her life was like. Sometimes they even seem to have their own personality.

Trophies

Trophies are beautiful works of art with a history. They are usually personalized with the name of the award, recipient, and date. My "best developed man" trophy is my personal favorite. Who doesn't love a well-developed man?

Books

Old books can be fascinating, and they are a versatile item to add to most rooms. They can be stacked in a bookcase, used as a riser beneath other objects, or used by themselves. I use them all over the house.

Bottles

Bottles look great almost anywhere. They come in a variety of sizes, so you can usually find the size you need if you know where to look.

Linens

Old linens fascinate me. Some have lace, some are monogrammed, and still others are decorated with beautiful hand-stitching. They are wonderful used as table runners, made into pillowcases, or just stacked in a cabinet.

Baskets

Baskets add lovely texture, and they too are versa-tile. They can be interesting on their own, but they also provide storage for many different types of items.

Hats

Old hats are intriguing to me because they make me wonder about the people who wore them. What did the person look like? Where did he or she live? What was that person's life like?

Paintings

Paintings are fun to display because they too seem per-sonal—someone created it.

A hat is interesting because it seems so personal.

Paintings can be pricey, so I don't have too many. I especially love portraits. Is it just me? I have a fascination with people, especially people who are long gone.

Silver

Vintage silver has a certain charm I can't deny. No matter what your taste is, there are so many different patterns available, and there are probably one or two that will appeal to you. The best part about vintage silverware is that you can actually use it, not just look at it. I love the bling of the silver and the craftsmanship.

Dishes

Vintage dishes, like vintage silver, come in many, many different patterns. You can find them in about any color or pattern you prefer. When displaying or using the dishes, you can stick to a matched set or mix and match.

Displaying Collections

Only collect what you love. I personally would never buy art as an investment. Some people do make money selling artwork, but from what I hear, it is rare. Why waste time collecting something you don't like, especially if you probably won't make money on it later? Collect what has meaning to you.

I think collections are fun, and even if you collect the same thing as someone else, your collection will be unique to you because your taste will influence the contents of the collection. Think of what you like and what you can afford to collect. Then buy only the best that you can afford.

I collect dishes. At first I wasn't picky. I picked up many dishes at garage sales that I didn't really like that much, but I bought them because they were cheap. Then I inherited a lot of dishes. I had literally hundreds of dishes. I had no idea how much I had, I just knew it was too much. And so I did the right thing, I gave a lot away. I kept the best ones but gave away the ones that I didn't really care about. That was at least half of the collection. I even sold a few. My collection became better, more refined—more of a collection and less of a stockpile. For the most part, I kept the dishes made in the US, France, Portugal, England, and Italy.

This smaller collection made more sense to me. It's not about having a lot of something, but rather about having a curated collection that makes you smile.

Once you begin collecting, the next issue is how to display the collection. You could store it in boxes, in the attic or basement, but what is the point of having a collection if you can't or don't display it? If it is in a box, you will forget about it and not enjoy it. I don't enjoy just knowing I have a collection of hand-painted French dishes. I want to handle them, see them, and use them.

Collections can sometimes grow out of hand and overwhelm a space. So how can they be dis-played beautifully in a room? One of the best ways to dis-play a rather large grouping is in a bookcase, in glass-front cabinets, or in a cupboard. For smaller collections, you will have many more options. For displaying linens or towels, try using a vintage wooden ladder.

Smaller collections can often be organized into a tray. They can also be grouped together on a desktop, chest, book-case, or inside a cabinet.

Personally, I prefer mine to look neat and orderly. If you have a collection of small items sitting on a desktop, it can look cluttered and jumbled. Small things display better if they are all contained into a cupboard or cabinet.

Grain sacks hung on a vintage ladder.

CHAPTER 7: ANTIQUE FURNITURE

Antiques have a past and a history; they are the keeper of secrets. Yes, they are usually imperfect, with a scratch here and a dent there, but slight signs of age make them so much more appealing to me. They usually have a patina that is impossible to replicate, especially on painted pieces. New furniture just doesn't have the detail and usually isn't as well built as antique furniture. Hand-carved detail is becoming a thing of the past. I also am a bit of a romantic and like to think about who owned the furniture, how the owners used the furniture, and what the original owners were like. Well-made furniture seems harder and harder to find. Now there is competition to make furniture cheaper and cheaper, so the focus is no longer on craftsmanship but on profit margins. Furniture is now made in a much more simple style, without hand carving or much detail. When I find a manufacturer that does include those beautiful details, the cost of the furniture is often quite high.

Manufacturers are competing on price with cheaply made, imported furniture. That is a recipe for cheap, mass-produced, unimaginative furniture. If a craftsman spends too much time on a chair, he can't sell it, because the buyer can go down the street to buy a much cheaper model. The bottom line is that people are not willing to pay for craftsmanship anymore. More and more, I turn to vintage and antique furniture to find those details I crave. Happily (for us), young people in Europe are selling family heirlooms to buy new furniture. Many think the old furniture isn't in step with modern life. That's sad for them but happy for those of us looking to buy the old furniture.

I buy up all I can. Hand-carved walnut wood makes my heart go pitter-patter. Yes, often these pieces need to be refreshed. The chairs often need new upholstery or the seat bottoms are broken. If I can do the repair or have it done without a ridiculous expense, I go for it.

Here are some things to keep in mind when buying antique furniture:

1. Look the piece over for previous damage and repairs, especially bad repair jobs.

Any repair job will reduce the value of the piece. A poor repair will reduce the value much more than a professional one. A previous repair will not keep me from buying a piece; it just depends on how obvious the repair is.

2. Check the back and bottom.

Does the piece look really dirty on the bottom and back? Often, repair work can only be seen on the back or bottom. These are places that hint at the age of the piece. Dirt and wear indicate a much older piece. Clean, smooth, straight areas indicate something much newer.

3. Open the drawers, open the doors, sit in the chairs, and try the latches.

You want to check to be sure drawers open easily. Chairs need to be able to hold the weight of people sitting in them. Latches, pulls, and handles should be sound.

4. Check to see if any locks have keys that go with them.

It is nice to get the key to a piece, but I have bought pieces missing their keys.

5. Ask for any information the owner has about the piece.

Sometimes they can tell you about the history of the piece, but most of the time they don't know. Still, if you don't ask, you probably won't get any information.

6. Inspect the joints on the drawers.

Are the drawer joints dovetail? If not, then the piece is probably new. Are the dovetail joints uniform? Uniform joints mean the piece is probably machine made and newer. Nonuniform joints appear on handmade and older pieces.

7. Are there any screws in the piece?

Metal screws indicate a newer piece, although the screw could just be a repair.

8. Do the nails look new or very old?

The older the nails look, the older the piece likely is.

9. Has the hardware or anything else on the piece been replaced?

If it has been replaced, that will probably affect the value, but it wouldn't necessarily keep me from buying it. Missing hardware can often be replaced.

10. Does the piece appear handmade or machine-made?

How uniform is it? To answer this question, you will need to see the bottom and the back of the piece. I once bought a table that looked old, but I didn't realize how old it was until I saw the bottom of the table. It had been scraped by hand. A chair I bought has one leg noticeably more narrow than the others. It is clearly made by hand. The more uniform and neat the piece, the newer it probably is.

11. Is the seller asking a reasonable price?

Answering this question requires a bit of research. What is the going rate for similar items in your area? Prices can vary greatly by geographical areas. Large cities are often known for having higher prices, but even within a city, prices can vary depending on street and neighborhood. Find out what you could buy a similar piece for somewhere else.

12. Is there any room to negotiate a better price?

13. If the owner won't come down on the price, will he or she deliver for free?

14. If it is a mirror, is the edge of the glass (on the back side) smooth or jagged?

15. If it is a mirror, how is the glass held in place?

16. Are all of the surfaces uniform and machine finished? (Anything that makes the furniture look like it was made by hand versus machinery is going to date the piece older.)

17. Is the piece one of a kind?

If the piece is unusual, then it will be difficult to determine what it should sell for. And if you are crazy in love with it, then maybe it is worth paying more for the piece rather than waiting to find a cheaper version somewhere else. I will pay a lot more for a special piece. I used to be more budget conscious and wouldn't pay much of a premium for a special piece. Now I appreciate those unusual pieces a lot more.

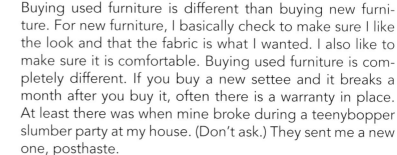

Buying used furniture is different than buying new furniture. For new furniture, I basically check to make sure I like the look and that the fabric is what I wanted. I also like to make sure it is comfortable. Buying used furniture is completely different. If you buy a new settee and it breaks a month after you buy it, often there is a warranty in place. At least there was when mine broke during a teenybopper slumber party at my house. (Don't ask.) They sent me a new one, posthaste.

If you buy used furniture, don't expect to get your money back or even any sympathy if it breaks or you change your mind. It is pretty much "buyer beware." Car and home sellers may have to disclose defects, but there is no such requirement on furniture so far as I know. The good news is that old furniture tends to be more solid and sturdy. The problem with breakage comes because the furniture is old and can have loose joints, torn fabric, dents, scratches, chips, gouges, and major repairs. To really inspect the piece, you need to turn it over and look at the bottom. Check for previous repairs. One time, I saw a chair leg that had broken off completely and was bolted back together in the most Frankenstein-like fashion; it was a bit creepy. The leg wasn't even straight anymore but was bent in an awkward, painful-looking way. Look the item over carefully. Ask questions of the seller. Ask if the seller knows of any specific damage.

If I am considering buying a chair, I sit in it and notice what happens next. Hopefully, nothing happens. Does it creak when I sit in it? Does it feel like it is about to give way? Gently push the back of the chair forward and back. Are the joints loose? My daughter was sitting in an antique chair I put in her room when she was a teenager. Over time, it began to give way, and the legs began to spread a bit more each day. An adult would have realized that the chair could no longer be trusted in its present condition, and stopped

using it. Being a teenager, she continued to use it until one day, *splat!* The chair broke apart from the seat, and she toppled to the floor. I was able to repair it later, but I don't really trust it anymore. It is now a glorified towel holder in our bathroom.

Now that we have discussed furniture warning signs, let's talk about some problems you might notice that are not a major issue. Either they are fixable or are something that is not a big deal. If you don't like the paint or stain, that is one of the easiest fixes. Remember, the piece can almost always be painted. (However, this may change the resale value if you plan on selling it later. I'll explain this later.) Changing the upholstery and slipcovering are a bit more complicated.

Here is a list of signs I look for that tell me to walk away from an antique piece of furniture:

1. Wobbly legs

2. Major obvious repairs

3. I'm afraid to sit on it

4. Legs that have been previously broken and glued back together

5. Smoke odor

6. Ridiculously high price

7. Too big for the space

While we are talking about what to look for in antique furniture, let's talk about what is considered normal wear. Antiques, by definition, are over one hundred years old. Most things over a hundred years old that have been used consistently will show some wear and age. For antique chairs or tables, that means there will be scratches. There might be a deep scratch or even a gouge. You will need to decide what is acceptable damage and wear and what is not. Repairs will also affect value, but again, I wouldn't buy the piece based on its resale value but whether the piece appeals to you. For example, the chair I mentioned that broke in my daughter's room is hand-carved and a real beauty. Some people would have said it wasn't worth keeping and thrown it out. I repaired it by screwing the legs to the seat. It isn't the best repair, but now it is usable. I suspect it wasn't worth much to begin with, but I love the carving on the back of the chair, and so have kept it. My husband sat in it recently before I could stop him, and it actually held his weight. I was a bit surprised and pleased. I am not keeping it because of its value but because I love it.

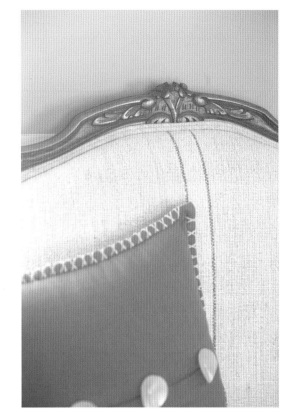

On the other hand, there are plenty of antiques worth a lot of money that I just find ugly and wouldn't buy for any reason. Some readers told me not to paint my chair because it would affect the value. If it were a rare antique, then, yes, they are absolutely correct. But for a non-valuable antique, updating it makes its appeal much broader and sometimes increases its value. Value is based on what people are willing to pay for something. If the piece appears out of style, even if it is in original condition, fewer people will want it, and thus it has less market value. (There are exceptions to this rule, of course.) I wouldn't forgo painting something just because it is old. It really depends on how I feel about the piece. (If you think the piece might be worth something, please check with an expert before painting it.)

Acceptable Problems

This is a list of problems that would not keep me from buying a piece of furniture, and I'll show you how to make some of these repairs in later chapters.

1. Ugly upholstery (fix: reupholster)

2. Broken caned seat (fix: repair caning or make new seat)

3. Ugly paint color (fix: paint)

4. Ugly wood stain (fix: paint or refinish)

5. Missing hardware (fix: replace hardware)

6. Torn leather (fix: reupholster)

7. Lost key (fix: don't lock it)

8. Light scratches and dents (fix: ignore or use a finish-restoring product to disguise scratches)

9. Worm holes (fix: ignore, unless it is an active infestation. How do you tell? One way to check is to put a white paper or sheet under the furniture and check it a few days later. If there are bits of insects there or fresh sawdust, you'll want to seek expert advice.)

CHAPTER 8: HOW TO PAINT & DISTRESS FURNITURE

I often buy sad, discarded furniture that the owner no longer wants. These pieces often need paint, new upholstery, or a new seat. I will take just about anything with good bones. I draw the line at wobbly or obviously broken furniture, but otherwise I am not too picky so long as it is beautiful.

If the piece has good bones but is covered in a less-than-stellar fabric, I will send it off with fabric to be re-covered. Often that is all that is needed to make a chair right as rain. Some people do this step themselves, and I applaud them for it, but I will happily pay. There are some things that just aren't worth losing your sanity for, and upholstery is one of them (at least for me).

Now, this chair was a complete trifecta of junk. The seat was broken; the stain was dark and shiny, and the cushion was undersized for the seat. I knew that with a new seat, paint, and a new cushion, this piece would shine. I don't know how to re-cane furniture, but I do know how to use a saw. Here's how I redid my chair:

Repairing the Seat

1. Measure the seat, and cut a piece of newspaper to fit it.

2. Place the newspaper on the seat to fine-tune the size, cutting around the arm supports.

3. Trim the newspaper to make it slightly bigger than the caned part of the seat, but not much bigger. It needs to reach the sturdy wood part of the seat so the wood frame supports the new seat. Make sure to allow a lot of room for chair arms if there are any. This is accomplished by trimming just a bit at a time, but be sure not to overtrim. After a few minutes, it should fit the chair seat pretty closely. This newspaper is now your pattern.

4. Place the newspaper pattern on thin plywood, and trace around it with a pencil.

5. Remove the paper after the image is traced onto the plywood.

6. Using a jigsaw, cut along the lines.

7. Place the new piece on your chair. Now you have a new support for your seat. This piece sits on top of the chair seat and supports the weight of a person. I am not opposed to repairing the seats—I actually recommend it; I simply don't have time right now to get the chairs repaired. And if someone over ninety pounds sits in the seat, I want to know the seat will hold that person.

Even with caned seats in good condition, I almost always reinforce them in this way, just to be safe. If you use a cushion, no one will know, and your seat is protected. Using the board doesn't hurt the chair, and it actually protects the caned seat.

Paint the Chair

This technique requires that you use chalky paint or homemade chalky paint. If you haven't heard of it before, you might be wondering why this paint is preferred over latex. If you want to distress the piece by sanding it, then the latex paint must cure for days before distressing. If you try to distress it as soon as it dries, the paint ends up peeling off, which is not the look you want. Also, if you are using latex paint, if you paint over a previously unpainted surface, you really should prime the piece first. Chalky paint does not require priming. And if your piece has been waxed, the wax must be removed before you paint with latex paint, but not with chalky paint. Also, chalky paint is flat, which is the look most people want in this situation. These directions are for use with chalky paint, not latex or oil-based paint.

If you prefer to make your own paint, you can do that as well. Mix about ¼ cup warm water with 3 tablespoons calcium carbonate powder, and stir until the calcium carbonate is dissolved. Calcium carbonate can be purchased at a health food store or ordered from Amazon.com. (Some people use plaster of Paris or unsanded grout instead of calcium carbonate.) Next, mix in 1 cup latex paint. Once it is fully incorporated, use the paint as you would latex paint. However, no sanding or priming is required for this homemade paint.

1. Clean the chair with a damp cloth. It's important, even when using chalky paint, to begin with a clean surface.

2. Check to see if your furniture has been previously painted with lead-based paint. If the piece was made before 1978, and it is painted, assume the paint contains lead. You can also purchase a lead test kit to ascertain if your painted piece was painted with lead-based paint.

3. If you suspect your piece has lead-based paint on it, please check with the EPA on the best way to address the potential health hazards. Addressing health issues is beyond the scope of this book, but please do your research and be safe. Now, assuming you are not working with lead-based paint, proceed.

4. If the piece has previously been painted and the paint is not lead-based, check it for loose paint. Any loose paint will need to be removed. This can be done with sandpaper or a brush.

5. Open the can of chalky paint and stir, or you can use your own homemade chalky paint.

6. For this chair, I used "chawk paint" from Southern Honey, color Stanley. Apply a first coat of paint like you would if you were using latex paint.

7. Allow the paint to dry between coats of paint.

8. Apply a second coat of paint. In most cases, two coats of paint will be sufficient. Apply a third only if needed.

Distress the Chair

Some people will not want to distress the paint finish, and that is totally up to you. If you choose not to distress the paint finish, you will need to add a coat of clear wax to protect the finish. If you do desire to add an antiqued finish, here is how you can do it:

HOW TO PAINT & DISTRESS FURNITURE

1. If you are new to this technique, I suggest you use a practice board first. A practice board is simply an extra piece of wood that you can paint, wax, and distress to see if you are happy with your paint color, distressing, and waxing technique. If you don't like how it looks, keep practicing until you find a technique that gives you the desired effect.

2. Lightly sand in areas that might have shown natural wear, like corners that might have knocked against a wall or arms that might have been used repeatedly. Oversanding or sanding in places that would not have shown wear will make it obvious this piece has been artificially distressed.

3. Wipe away the loose sawdust from the piece.

4. Select a wax you will use to finish the piece. If the paint is not too light, you can use an antiquing wax, meaning a brownish wax. If you do not want to use wax to antique the finish or if the piece is white, I suggest you use a clear wax. I use Southern Honey wax for the clear wax. My current favorite antiquing wax is HowardWax in Walnut. If you use tinted antiquing wax, keep in mind that this wax is brown, so it will change the look of the paint, making it darker and more yellow. Test the effect in an inconspicuous spot to make sure you like it. One thing you can do if you are concerned the wax will be too dark is to do a first coat of wax with clear wax. Then apply a coat of tinted wax. If you don't like the tinted wax, it will be much easier to remove if there is a clear coat of wax underneath. The darker wax can be removed to some extent by buffing with a cloth. If you want to remove more, use sandpaper.

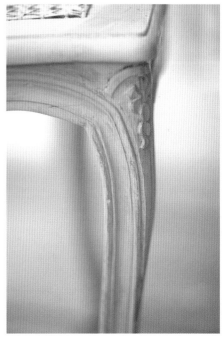

5. Apply the wax by dabbing a stiff bristled brush into the wax can, and then brushing it on your piece. I recommend using a wax brush. If you use a cloth to apply the wax, you will waste a lot of wax. For areas with hand carving, you'll need to use a jabbing motion to get the wax into the deep recesses.

6. Once you have applied the wax to an area the size of two pieces of bread, use a soft cloth to remove the excess wax and buff the area.

7. Continue until you finish waxing and buffing the entire piece.

I have used this technique for years on many pieces of furniture. I used the same technique on this next chair. The chair had been broken but I couldn't stand to part with it. I added some screws to the legs so the chair could be used again. Then I decided some paint would make it even lovelier. I painted not only the wood but also the fabric seat on this chair.

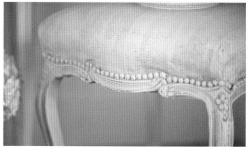

Detail of painted back and finished chair.

I've even used the same technique on this mirror. I added an extra layer of dry brushed paint to get the shade just right.

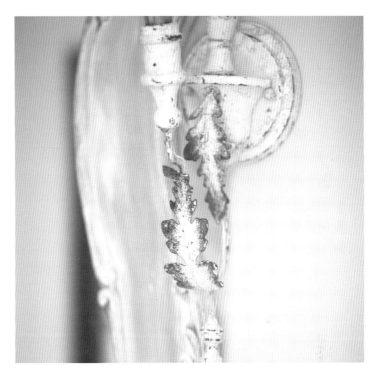

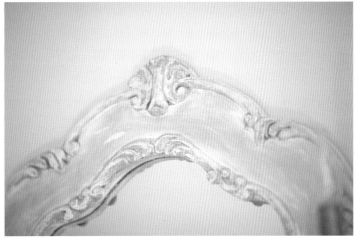

This antique cabinet was too dark before, but the finished product is light and airy.

CHAPTER 9: SLIPCOVERING
A DINING ROOM CHAIR

It starts with an innocent enough thought: "I think this would look nice slipcovered." From there, depending on the size of the project, I either go into "this is a piece of cake" mode or the dreaded, "Why, why, why? What was I thinking? This is sheer madness!" mode. I actually like sewing, but big sewing jobs can feel overwhelming, even to someone like me who has made many, many slipcovers. So my first recommendation is to start small. If you have never made a slipcover, don't start with a sofa or a wingback chair. They might cause you to break out in a cold sweat in the middle of the night. Let's say you have embraced your inner seamstress, and you have made the commitment to make a slipcover. Let's go through the steps to create a simple ruffled seat slipcover.

1. Buy a cushion.

For this chair, I just happened to have an extra seat cushion that fit perfectly. For dining room chairs, you should be able to find a cushion pretty close to the correct size. Don't worry about getting the prettiest one; it will be covered up anyway.

2. Determine the amount of fabric needed. (These small projects are pretty straightforward.)

    a. Measure the width and depth of the seat. Mine is 16 inches wide by 15 inches deep. Use the depth to determine how much fabric is needed for the seat section. For mine (15 inches deep), I add a ½-inch seam allowance all the way around the seat, meaning the depth needed was actually 16 inches.

        • Depth (15 inches) + seam allowance (½ inch) + seam allowance (½ inch) = *amount of fabric needed for seat (16 inches)*

    b. Next, you will need fabric for the ruffle. Determine the height of your ruffle. I chose 5 inches for my drop, or height of the ruffle. I then added a ½-inch seam allowance and 1 inch for the hem.

- Ruffle drop (5 inches) + hem (1 inch) + seam allowance (½ inch) = total ruffle height (6½ inches).

c. Next, take the tape measure around the outside edge of the entire seat, measuring the perimeter. My project had a 60-inch perimeter, or 60 inches long. Because the fabric will be ruffled at roughly double the length, I double that number and add a bit for good measure.

- Perimeter of the seat (60 inches) x 2 = 120. Add an extra 5 inches just to be safe, so 125 inches are needed.

d. Given the answers from the previous questions, we know that the ruffle fabric will be 125 inches long and 6½ inches high.

e. Divide the total length (125 inches) by the width of your fabric, which you may not have yet. Most are 54 inches wide or more. (125 inches ÷ 54 inches = 2.3 widths of fabric.)

f. That means we need 2.3 (round up to the next whole number), or 3 rows of a 6½-inch ruffle.

g. 3 rows x 6½-inch ruffle length = *19½ inches of fabric needed for the ruffle.*

h. Total amount of fabric needed for this project

- Amount of fabric needed for the seat + amount of fabric needed for the ruffle = total amount of fabric needed:

- 16 inches (needed for seat) + 19½ inches (needed for ruffle) = 35½ inches. I needed 1 yard (36 inches) for my project.

3. *Mark the fabric.* Place the cushion on top of the fabric. Make sure the cushion is sitting straight, not crooked. Be mindful of fabric patterns. Place the back of the cushion near the edge of the fabric. Draw a line around the outline of the cushion. If your fabric has a pattern, it is imperative that your fabric be straight from front to back.

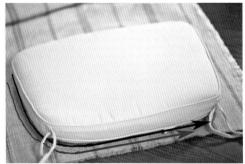

4. *Mark where you will cut.* In step 3 we drew an outline around the cushion (shown in black). That line does not include the seam allowance. We need to draw a new line that is ½-inch bigger than the original outline that was drawn. The new outline is shown in maroon.

5. *Cut the fabric.* Using the outside (maroon) lines you drew, and cut the fabric.

6. *Fold the fabric.* Fold the fabric in half to be sure the fabric is symmetrical. Trim the bigger side so that the pattern is symmetrical on both sides.

7. *Cut the fabric for the ruffle.* Measure a strip the length of fabric from selvage edge to selvage edge. For my project, I used 6½ inches for the width of the fabric. Mark and cut this strip of fabric. Make sure to cut strips until you have enough for your project. For this project I needed 3 lengths of fabric, so I cut three strips of 6½ inch-wide fabric.

8. *Sew the pieces of ruffle together, end to end.*

9. *Press open the seams with an iron.*

10. *Fold up one edge of the ruffle with a ½-inch fold, and press with the iron.*

11. *Fold over the folded edge one more time with a ½-inch fold and then use the iron to press in place.*

12. *Sew the hem.*

13. *Use a ruffler to make the ruffle.* I set mine on it to make a ruffle every 6 stitches. I also set the stitch for a distance ½ inch from the edge of the fabric.

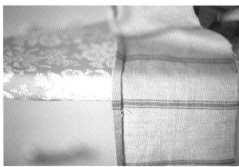

14. *Place seat fabric on the chair and pin, right sides together. Pin ruffle onto the seat fabric. Pin along the seat fabric.*

15. *Leave gaps in the ruffle to allow room for the back of the chair.* (Like where the back of the chair attaches to the seat.)

16. *Sew the ruffle onto seat, removing pins as you go.*

17. *Press ruffle down in place using iron.*

18. *Place the seat cushion on the chair, and place slip-cover on top.*

I did not add ties for the slipcover, but you could add some if desired.

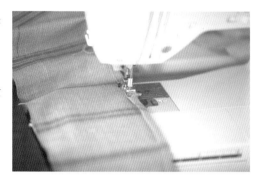

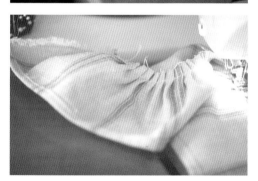

CHAPTER 10: FUN PROJECTS

Are you a "crafty" person? The kind of person who can take a toilet paper roll and make it look like an expensive napkin ring for a fancy dinner? That is not me. I am *not* crafty. However, I have a few projects that were really quite simple and fun to do. I know if I can do these, so can you.

Chalkboard from a Screen Door

Talk about fun—I loved working on this chalkboard! I asked my builder where I could find a screen door. He said he was getting ready to throw one out, and I could have it if I wanted it. It wasn't exactly what I had in mind, but I knew it had potential. It even fit in my SUV! Here are the steps I went through to make the chalkboard:

1. Remove the screen and (in my case) the lattice that were added by the previous owner.

2. Paint the door a creamy white.

3. Pick up some lauan, at your local hardware store, and cut it to size.

4. Paint the lauan with chalkboard paint.

5. Attach the board to the back of the door using wood screws.

6. Cure the chalkboard paint for at least 2 days.

7. Take a piece of chalk and lay it flat against the board. Rub it all over the board until it is covered with chalk. This seasons the board. It took about 3 pieces of chalk to do the entire board.

8. Wipe off the excess chalk using a dry cloth. Do not use a wet cloth, or you will have to start all over again.

9. Add hanging hardware on the back, and you are done. It's a simple project, but it makes for a great statement piece.

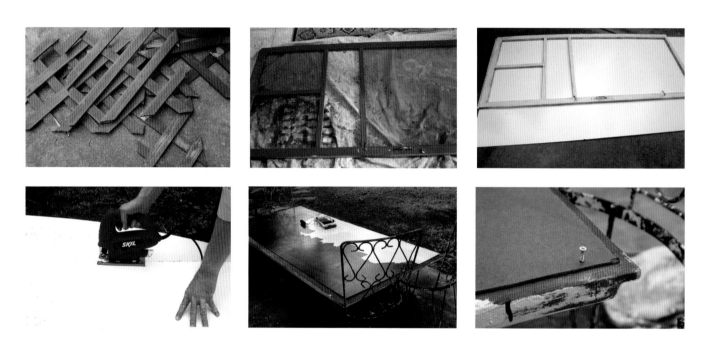

Converting a Crib to a Bench

I love taking something that might otherwise be discarded and making it into something new and fun. Old iron cribs really appeal to me, but I wouldn't want to put a real baby in one because it probably wouldn't be safe. I remade one into a bench instead.

For the Bench

1. Take the front side rail off of the crib. If you can't remove that side, then you might not be able to convert the crib. The side rail on my crib came off easily.

2. Add a piece of plywood cut to the size of the crib. (I did this because the bottom did not look like it would support the weight of an adult.) Cut the plywood so it extends past the crib framing. This way the frame supports the wood.

3. Buy a new mattress for the seat.

For the Mattress Cover

1. Measure the length and width of the mattress. (52 inches × 27 inches)

2. Cut 2 pieces of fabric to those dimensions (one for the top and one for the bottom), and add an inch for a seam allowance in each direction. The two pieces I cut were 53 inches × 28 inches.

3. Cut a long strip of fabric for the sides of the mattress. The width of the strip should be the height of the mattress plus an inch seam allowance.

The height of my mattress was 5 inches, so the strip of fabric needed to be 5 inches plus 1 inch for seam allowances, or 6 inches tall.

The width of the fabric was 54 inches, but I needed a fabric equal to twice the length plus twice the width. So I needed a piece with a length of 160 inches (two 52-inch pieces + two 28-inch pieces), plus seam allowances. I add 3 inches of seam allowances, so the total length of fabric I needed was 163 inches. From

this, I cut 3 pieces that were 54 inches by 6 inches. I sewed these end to end to make a 160-inch length of fabric to match the perimeter of the mattress.

4. Sew together the ends of your fabric, and press the seams open.

5. Pin the cushion top piece of fabric to the long 160-inch length of fabric that will be the sides of the cushion. Then sew the top to the side.

6. Pin the bottom to the sides, but leave one end open to insert the mattress.

7. Turn the mattress cover right side out.

8. Insert the mattress in the opening.

9. Finish the sewing by hand.

Bench

1. Place the board (already cut) on the bottom of the crib.

2. Add the mattress.

I could still see the board underneath the mattress when I looked at the front of the bench. A lace table runner tucked under the mattress covered the board and added a soft touch.

This project is pretty basic if you know how to sew and use a saw.

CHAPTER 11: TABLESCAPES

I love hosting parties not only because I love people, but also because I love food, dishes, flowers, silver, pretty glasses, and . . . you get the point. A pretty table makes any party more exciting and fun. Sadly, it is becoming more and more unusual to see parties where the hosts use real dishes. As a dish addict/fanatic/collector/connoisseur, I adore using my real dishes during parties. We recently had a party at our farm, where we set up tables end to end in the pasture. Most people would've used paper plates, and I tried—I really tried—to use paper plates, but I couldn't do it. It had to look pretty. Paper plates are not pretty; they are practical. I had always dreamed of having a long table in a field of wildflowers—a long table covered with a white tablecloth, with wildflowers in vases along the length of the table. I pictured friends sitting at the table, enjoying a meal, savoring the company and hearty fare. Children would be flying kites, teenagers would be taking off to explore the woods, and adults would be laughing. This was the scene for a party we held at the farm. The fields were a sea of blue as far as the eye could see. It was the kind of day that you don't want to end. We sat at the table, not wanting to leave, knowing that when someone stood, the spell would be broken.

Napkins

Sometimes I use bandanas for napkins. Bandanas make for nice, large cloth napkins that are great for messy foods. I also use tea towels for napkins. They, too, are big and great for a picnic with messy foods. I also use vintage linen napkins for dinners, and I have lots of cotton napkins for less formal affairs. I love using fabric napkins for special parties or dinners. They just make it feel so special. Yes, the napkins will need to be washed and probably ironed, but if you have a party once a year, that isn't a lot of time in the grand scheme of things. It is worth it!

Set out all your napkins so you can decide which ones go best with the dishes and tablecloth you have selected for the meal. If you have just one set of white napkins, then you are done with this step!

Dishes

I try to avoid paper plates unless it is a very, very casual picnic. I know not everyone agrees with me, but I prefer to use real dishes for meals. I don't think they have to be fancy dishes. I have a set of glass

plates we use when we have a big crowd at the farm, and I prefer those to paper. When guests see you have taken the extra time to make the event special, they will adore you for putting in the extra effort. It will feel like an extra-special party, and they will feel like they are important guests.

If variety is the spice of life, then my dishes are mighty spicy. I've got lots to choose from. I first have to know where we will eat, inside or outside. Once I know what table we will be eating at, I decide which dishes we will use. I love using a different set each day. When I host a tea, often each person gets a teacup with a different pattern. Some

people have accused me of having two houses just so I will have more room to store all of my dishes. That is entirely not true, although I do have a china cabinet on my back porch. *What? Is that wrong?* You can use dishes that match or mix different patterns for a more eclectic look.

If you don't have enough dishes for a party, there are a few things you can do. First, you can borrow dishes from your neighbors or family. You can also buy inexpensive

dishes. I bought some glass plates at IKEA for our wildflower party. They were about a dollar apiece, so if one broke or got lost in the pasture, I would not miss it. I also have a set of dishes I am not excited about any more. I started to sell them but decided they, too, would make great dishes for my back porch. Another place you can usually get a good deal on dishes is thrift or resale shops.

Bluebonnets, green flowers, and green apples make for a fresh centerpiece

Flatware

I love, love, love using silverware, and it is an important element of Farmhouse French style. Sterling is expensive, but you can still find great deals on silver-plate sets. And if you are willing to go with unmatched sets, you can get an even better deal. I also have some fun sets of flatware. There's a pink set, a black set, and a bronze set in addition to my stainless and silver-plate ware.

Tablecloth

If you don't have a lot of stuff like I do, the decision-making process will go fast. After I select the dishes, next comes the tablecloth. White linen is great and goes with everything, but I also love to use vintage tablecloths. I'm looking for a tablecloth that suits my mood and goes with the dishes I want to use. Other things you can use include burlap, shower curtains (yes, I have used a shower curtain before), curtains, drop cloths, fabric remnants, throws, and towels. I also use fabulous towels from Turkish T as tablecloths; the fringe adds a nice effect.

Glass creamer
full of vintage
spoons

Centerpiece

I use the dishes and tablecloth as a starting point for selecting my centerpiece. If you don't want to spend any money on flowers, you often don't have to. I usually look around and see if there is anything I can cut from my yard. If you want something specific, many times you can find something pretty at the grocery store. You can go to a florist, but a grocery store typically has less expensive but similar flowers.

If I am styling a table that won't be used for a meal, I take a different approach than if the table will be used. If the table will be used for dining, I avoid tall flowers or anything that might block faces and conversations across the table. A short individual vase on everyone's plate is nice and keeps the flowers low. Flowers should coordinate with your dishes and tablecloth. Look at all the colors and see if they look good together. Colors opposite on the color wheel often do well together.

How to set a table

If you are unsure about the basic table setting, you don't even need to buy an etiquette book anymore. Just look it up online. The bread plate goes on the left and the drink on the right. The fork goes on the left and spoon and knife on the right. The napkin can go to the left of the fork or in the glass or on the plate. For dessert, the fork or spoon, whichever is being used, will be above the plate. The fork will look like it was moved up there from the fork position on the left (that is

how I remember the position). So the tines should point to the right. The same thing goes for the dessertspoon. It is positioned as if it slid up from the right side of the plate, with the bowl of the spoon on the left. Alternately, you can provide the fork or spoon with dessert when it is served.

My mother-in-law used to organize the dinners for the board of regents and board of visitors for a major hospital system in Houston, so she knew where everything went on a table. I learned a lot from her, and that experience gave me great confidence when giving a dinner party.

Drink Station

You can ask each of the guests what they want and serve it to them or let them get their own drinks. I like the serve-yourself option. Guests can get what they want, when they want it, without having to feel like they are bothering the host or hostess. I have found that most people prefer this option.

Preparing the food

It's all about having fun with your guests, so I like to have all of my food cooked and ready to go before the guests arrive. I do almost all of my food prep before the big day so I am not in the kitchen during the party. If it is a big event, sometimes I cook for a week before and freeze items ahead of time. With today's busy schedules, ordering from a restaurant is a great option. Just be sure to serve guests from your own beautiful dishes and not Styrofoam containers. A few weeks before the party, I put a menu together, trying to use mostly dishes that can be prepared ahead of time. If I can make it and freeze it, even better. The night before the party, if I can, I set up the table for the event and set out the serving dishes I will be using with serving utensils.

Preparation for Event

The whole point of a party is to have fun and enjoy the time with your guests. If you end up in the kitchen the entire time or if things go wrong, it might not be much fun. That is why I try to be as organized as possible to make sure it will all go smoothly. A stressed hostess makes for an awkward party. Try to do as much as you can ahead of time so you can participate in your own party. Select your menu and which dishes (including serving dishes) you will use on your table a few weeks ahead of time. Do as much food prep as possible the day before or early the day of the party. Another tip is to cook only things you have already made in the past. Don't experiment when cooking for a crowd. You don't want any nasty surprises.

Dealing with Disaster

If you are prepared, organized, doing as much cooking as possible in advance of your event, and using tried-and-true recipes, you will minimize the chances of a disaster. For

At this party, I served macarons, meringues, and petit fours for dessert.

example, don't make soufflé, which can easily fall, unless you are a seasoned cook and know what you are doing.

Minor problems have a way of happening. You may run out of ice, an appetizer might burn, or you might have forgotten to salt a dish. Try to take all of this in stride. Your guests will be forgiving. Try not to call attention to it, just do the best you can. If you have to mention it, laugh it off. If it is bad, and you mention it, guests will feel the need to build you back up. Just move forward and fix things as best you can.

For big disasters, a different approach may be needed. If your roast is still raw or the dog eats your dessert, you will not be able to move forward and just ignore it. If the worst occurs, you can always explain what happened and order pizza or a cake at the bakery. It will make for quite the story back at the office the next day. Just try to have fun. Life is made up of experiences, and when things go wrong, I try to learn from them, and get a laugh. Mistakes aren't the end of the world. If you have invited good friends, they will be supportive of you if things do go wrong. Rarely have I seen such a disaster. Usually the problems are quite minor, and often go unnoticed by guests. Enjoy!

CHAPTER 12: THE KITCHEN, HEART OF THE HOME

The kitchen is one of the most important rooms in a home. This is the room where the family spends time preparing meals, and it is often where they share a meal as well. This is where guests tend to gather during parties, no matter how fancy the dining room is. A well-designed kitchen is not only a piece of art but is also functional. If you like to cook and bake like I do, then you probably spend a large chunk of time in the kitchen every day. Even if you don't cook much, you still might use a kitchen to heat up a take-out meal or to eat breakfast. Since you probably spend a good deal of time in here, it's important that you enjoy this room. And the more you enjoy it, the more time you will want to spend there. Even if you don't enjoy cooking, having a beautiful kitchen just might win you over to the joy of it. Chores like washing dishes are so much more tolerable in a pretty kitchen! (Or maybe that's just my opinion.)

There isn't just one look that says *Farmhouse French kitchen* to me. There are so many different kitchen touches that evoke a Farmhouse French attitude. You don't need to rip out your current kitchen and install a brand-new one to get French accents. It's amazing how adding this look in small doses still gives a room a big impact. Work with what you have to give your kitchen a fresh, exciting look. I have included some updates that are simple and inexpensive, along with some that are more involved and expensive. The list is not meant to be a definitive one but simply a list of suggestions and ideas to get you started.

I love the feel of a traditional country French kitchen with stone walls, open shelving, a farmhouse sink with a skirt, and a big pine table. Most of us don't have a kitchen like that. But that's okay. There are plenty of things we can incorporate into our kitchens to create a little French *je ne sais quoi*.

Decorating with Dishes

I adore dishes and have been collecting them since I was in college. I knew I had too many, but then my collection doubled when my mother-in-law passed away, leaving all of her dishes to my husband. She too was a collector of dishes. I was in a predicament. What was I going to do with over ten sets of dishes, along with many odd pieces? And on her deathbed (I am not making this up) she begged me to keep all of her good stuff. I patted her hand, smiled and told her I would do the best I could. After I left the room, I groaned. Four people need only so many dishes, and I was already way over my limit. I kept as many as I could, then sold and gave away what was left.

I was still overrun with dishes, so I had to get creative about how I displayed them. There are lots of ways to display dishes, and they are easy to incorporate into almost any room. I draw the line at the bathroom. Oh, I spoke too soon. I do keep a little teacup full of lavender in there.

Open shelving is perfect for storing dishes. To give a collection a cohesive look, I suggest you display dishes of just one color. White dishes are fabulous, and they look wonderful when displayed.

You can also display dishes in a wire shelf. I love this one with the white ironstone. Collecting things of all one color gives the collection a unifying theme.

I don't like to limit the display of dishes to the kitchen. I love to display them anywhere I can. I found a little cabinet at an auction that I use to display dishes. It wasn't until after I brought it home that I realized what it was—the top of any old grandfather clock case. Someone before me removed the clock itself and added a shelf. Now it is a funky way to show off extra teacups and other goodies.

Another way to display dishes is in a plate rack. You can go with all white or a mix of pattterns.

Kitchen Updates

I'm all about working with what you have, so I would never suggest you rip out your kitchen, unless that is what *you* want. So what can you do to make what you already have feel more updated? Here are a few ideas. I've broken them down by financial investment, from expensive updates to budget-conscious updates. Some of the ideas are more elegant and others, rustic.

Expensive Updates

1. *Paint cabinets white.* It may be considered a trend, but I do think it is a good solution for updating a kitchen. Some stained cabinets end up looking dated. I love the look of stained cabinets, but they often go out of style faster than white cabinets.

2. *Change out the backsplash.* Subway tile is a great way to go. My suggestion is to go simple and neutral. You probably won't be in this house forever, and a trendy tile could seriously date your kitchen and reduce its value down the road.

3. *Add new countertops.* Marble is stunning and gorgeous, but can be impractical for people who actually use their kitchen. If you want a similar look that doesn't etch or stain as easily, you can try white granite or quartzite. If you really want marble, try the honed version. If the marble becomes etched, it won't be as obvious. Be sure to invest in a good sealant, as well as to minimize staining.

4. *Reface cabinets.* This option doesn't require the entire cabinet to be replaced. It simply adds a thin veneer to the cabinets and replaces the doors and drawer fronts.

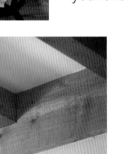

5. *Add beams.* They seem to have universal appeal. Here is what I noticed in my home. When we have visitors, most of them comment about how much they like the beams. The strange thing is how the beams have such a chameleon effect. People that like English style tell me they look so "Tudor." Someone from Alaska said the beams reminded him of home, and my fellow Francophiles think they look French. That may explain why many people like them. The beams say *cozy* and *warm* no matter what your preferred style is.

For those of us who love French style, the exposed beams really give a home a Farmhouse French feel. We found our reclaimed beams at a salvage yard nearby. They still have bits of paint on them here and there. If you love the look and are lamenting the lack of beams in your house, did you know they can usually be added later? And for probably less than you think? Except for the large beam down the middle of our kitchen, our beams are purely cosmetic. Check with an engineer to ensure your home can support the additional weight. If you already have crown molding now, that will probably need to be removed.

6. *Update appliances.* Stainless is usually the safest bet for resale, though there are some charming vintage-looking appliances in various colors available on the Internet.

7. *Change out your vent hood.* You can go with something rustic and fun like this old awning or something more traditional.

8. *Add a plate rack.* I asked my carpenter to add big plate racks on either side of my breakfast room window, but you can add a much smaller plate rack and still get a big impact.

9. *Update doorknobs.* For doorknobs, I chose crystal knobs with a curvy plate. I love the idea of using antique doorknobs, but if you do, keep in mind you probably won't be able

to find a full matching set for your home. I used new knobs, so they all match.

10. *Add built-in open shelving.* These are great for displaying dishes, crystal, silver, or any other thing you want to show off.

11. *Convert some of your cabinet doors to glass-front doors.* I love the look of the glass doors. It is a great way to show off your dishes without exposing them to dust.

12. *Update the bar or counter stools.* These stools may seem too fancy for a kitchen, but why not? The fabric is actually an easy-care synthetic that resists stains. So you can have something French and lovely that is also comfortable and practical.

Budget-Conscious Updates

1. *Clean off your countertops.* Having fewer things sitting out is a no-cost solution that really makes your kitchen look better.

2. *Update lighting and add a chandelier where you can.* This might require an electrician, although I've changed out many a light fixture by myself. Light fixtures can look dated after a while. When you change them out, look for something that you love!

3. *Add removable shelving.* This can be done using boards and brackets to display dishes or by adding a premade shelving unit. This type of shelving is not permanent and can be removed when you move. Another plus is that it can often be added by the homeowner.

4. *Use baskets for storage.* Here the homeowner used a large basket to hold cookie sheets and other kitchen supplies.

5. *Use vintage scales.* I suppose you could use them to actually weigh ingredients, but I like to use them for decor purposes only.

6. *Add some ironstone.* I love to use ironstone in decor. Setting out an ironstone pitcher or platter adds a special touch in just about any kitchen.

7. *Add a bottle drying rack.* These were originally made to dry wine bottles, but they work great to display mugs, cups, and glasses. The vintage ones can be pricey, but (happily) reproduction bottle drying racks are available at much lower prices.

8. *Use pretty vintage containers to hold silverware.*

9. *Use something unexpected as your spoon rest.* I use a pretty plate or pressed glass bowl. I have yet to see a spoon rest that I like. So why not find something pretty in your cupboard and make it work as a spoon rest?

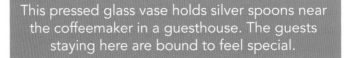

This pressed glass vase holds silver spoons near the coffeemaker in a guesthouse. The guests staying here are bound to feel special.

10. *Add some fun vintage accessories.* These could include rolling pins, old utensils, or collectibles.

11. *Add enamelware.* The enamelware pitchers from France have a unique look with an inverted cone shape, while their American cousins have more of an hourglass shape. I personally like both.

12. *Update the cabinet pulls.* Cabinet pulls are easy to replace. Usually the process takes minutes per pull or knob and requires just a screwdriver. The cost per pull or knob varies greatly, but those on a budget can usually find something nice for a reasonable price.

13. *Use old silver or ironstone pitchers to hold your spoons and whisks.* It's okay if the silver gets a bit tarnished. It's called patina. I leave plastic spatulas in the drawer and display the stainless and wood utensils in my pitcher for aesthetic reasons.

14. *Store ripening fruit in pretty bowls or containers.* It seems we often have fruit sitting about in our kitchen as we wait for it to ripen. My philosophy is, why not display that fruit in a pretty bowl? When you skip the plastic bowl and use a bowl from your collection, it goes from practical storage to a work of art.

15. *Add a piece of furniture to your kitchen.* If your kitchen is small, you probably won't be able to add any furniture. But if you can, it gives your kitchen a warm, cozy feel, like an old kitchen before the days of built-in cabinets.

16. *Display only dishes of one color in your kitchen.* I had dishes of all colors in my cabinets because I collect all sorts of dishes. But then I tried moving all of those dishes out and just put in white dishes. And guess what happened? I loved it! It looks better because all of the dishes now look like they belong to the same collection.

Round Top Rustic Kitchen

This rustic kitchen is full of charm. The homeowner nailed her Texas Farmhouse French look. Tucked away down a sleepy dirt road, this abode works as a charming weekend getaway home. What it lacks in size, it more than makes up in style. This homeowner took the time to incorporate lots of reclaimed materials. The beams, walls, reclaimed cabinetry, flooring, shelving, and even the island are all made from reclaimed materials.

The cabinetry has been sealed so there is no need to worry about the paint peeling. The island is my favorite part of this kitchen. It's gorgeous in its simplicity. You rarely see a pot filler over the stove in such a compact kitchen, so this one is a rare luxury.

The walls are covered in shiplap, the island is topped with wood, and the counters are marble. It's amazing how much character they added in such a tiny space.

Guest Cottage

This is yet another small kitchen packed with charm. This guest cottage is also full of reclaimed materials and is oozing with warmth and fun. It's casual and beckons guests to come in and make themselves at home.

Dishes openly displayed like these vintage white ironstone pieces provide character. Using open shelving similar to this wire shelf is a great way to add storage to a small kitchen.

Elegant Farm Kitchen

The boards on this kitchen's island and the basket pendant light provide warm farmhouse details to this upscale city kitchen. A long antique farmhouse table is perfect for the empty-nester owners and works well in the space, while the large gas stove provides ample room to cook.

Using antiques in the kitchen warms up the space and makes it cozy.

A pretty soup tureen gives the table color and character.

The Blue Kitchen

This charming kitchen is warm and unique with its blue cabinets and AGA stove—an unusual sight in Texas. The beams add a rustic touch to this English-styled kitchen. The cooper sink gives the room warmth and character.

One of the best features of this kitchen is how it opens up to this incredible courtyard.

Guest Quarters Kitchen

This studio apartment is perfectly sized for one person. It's currently used as guest quarters but could be a full-time apartment. The white subway tile and quartzite countertop gives the kitchen a new feel. The refrigerator is full-sized. A vintage Italian-made Louis XV card table works beautifully in such a small space.

Cozy Guest Kitchenette

This kitchenette works in a small space set up for guests. With just a sink, a tiny fridge, and a microwave, guests are set for an overnight stay. Silverware sits in a little crystal vase ready for guests to make their own fresh cup of coffee.

My City Kitchen

The reason we ended up building a new house rather than buying an existing one comes down to the kitchen, pure and simple. I wanted this exact kitchen and couldn't find a home with this look. I wanted it to be open to the living room, to have a separate breakfast room, a big island, large refrigerator, glass-front cabinets, farmhouse sink, a butler's pantry with open shelving, plate racks, and a forty-eight-inch gas range. As the plan evolved, we added the rustic beamed ceiling, the crackle subway tile and the white granite. This combination kitchen and living room is by far the biggest space in the house, and it is where we hang out as a family. I wanted something elegant yet cozy—something grand yet inviting. I knew we would have to work to make the room with lots of white and ten-foot ceilings feel cozy. Rustic beams and tiles with a hint of color helped to warm the space. Plates in the plate rack, a big stove, and comfy stools at the counters gave the room the feeling of a warm embrace.

CHAPTER 13: DINING SPACES

Some people feel the idea of a dining room is completely outdated. I still really like the idea of a dining room because it is a place set aside for meals with family and friends. Notice I didn't say *formal* dining room. I don't feel it has to be formal, but I like having a nice-sized space for dining. It is great to have a place to entertain. There is nothing wrong with eating in the kitchen or breakfast room; the dining room is usually bigger so it can accommodate more people. I like to have a space that will accommodate not only my family of four but also a few other people. Whatever the configuration in your home, it's about making it comfortable for you and your family. I strongly believe having meals together is important to a family, so it is a passion of mine to create spaces that embrace lingering at the table and continuing conversation. If it is unwelcoming, people will be in a hurry to leave, and that does not encourage long conversations. Chairs need to be comfortable, and the space needs to be inviting. I want the space to be soft but lively, beautiful but approachable, elegant but not stuffy. In short, I want it to be big on elegance and style while, at the same time, comfortable and cozy.

Common Dining Room Mistakes

1. Table Too Big for the Space

All too often, I see tables that are too big for the dining room. If you have to hold in your breath to squeeze past the table, it's too tight. Feeling jammed into a corner is not conducive to lingering.

2. Too Formal

Beautiful is one thing, formal and stiff is another. You want your dining room to be inviting. If your room seems too formal, try adding some warm elements. Include casual touches to tone it down, like baskets, crates, rustic fabrics, or wood. Vintage items can also help make the space feel cozy. You want your guests to relax, not feel like if they touch something it will break.

3. Window Coverings Are Dated

Sometimes when we spend a lot of money on something, it's difficult to get rid of it when it isn't working for us anymore. I think older window treatments can fall into that category. If the window treatments are dated in the dining room, they will not invite lingering. For dining rooms with dated window coverings, you can simply remove them and leave the windows bare. Or you can hang some simple premade sheers for a soft look.

4. Too Matchy-Matchy

I prefer to have an assortment of pieces that look like they were collected over time. Usually my chairs don't match the table. If you have a table, chairs, and a china cabinet that all match, you might want to consider changing something out. I rarely see china cabinets even used much anymore.

Breakfast Room

 A mix of the rustic with the refined is a look I lean towards in decor. This corner of our home houses a lovely antique French armoire that I had converted to a china cabinet. The silvering on the mirror was removed so it is clear now, and we added shelves. It is juxtaposed against the rustic antique beams and the casual French lantern. The table and chairs are also casual antique country French. I used fabulous blue seat cushions to add some soft color to the room.

The built-in plate racks also add interest to this breakfast room. Plates can be changed out with the seasons. Rotate your favorite plates for a new look whenever you like. It also provides much-needed storage for large platters.

Round Top Farmhouse

For this open-concept Round Top farmhouse, casual is the way to go. The look is relaxing, with a hint of elegance. A large demijohn, an ironstone pitcher, and simple linen table runner give the room rustic appeal. The antique table is also perfectly beautiful.

The burlap host chairs are comfortable and add wonderful texture to the room.

Shiplap boards and beams give the wall loads of texture and interest without making the room feel busy.

City Dining Room

In this dining room, I used grays and whites, with just a touch of blue (in the wool rug). I used a cascading effect with the mirror in the back down to the console against the back wall, the back chairs, the dining room table, the bench, and then to the floor. Using a bench at the table makes the room feel much more open because you can see the entire table. The glass bottles add height without making the room feel closed off because they are transparent.

On the side wall, a Mora clock adds lots of interest with a very small footprint. It is as visually appealing as a piece of furniture might be, but it doesn't take up too much space in the dining room. There is plenty of clearance around the table. The map of Paris adds appeal to the wall, without adding jarring colors. The neutrals of the art blend right in with the other neutrals in this dining room.

On another wall, I placed vintage tole candle sconces surrounded by antique gesso frames. I think the frames are a work of art on their own.

Rather than using a traditional china hutch, I used a rustic console to add an unexpected twist to the dining room. Think of things that will work well together but aren't matched. The vintage French chairs don't match the table, but they work well together.

Vintage sconces framed by antique gesso frames.

Tip: If you don't like your table but can't afford to replace it, try using a tablecloth to disguise it.

Tip: After fresh flowers are spent, tie a string around them and hang them upside down to dry. When fully dried, place them in a container. After a while, if you have enough, place them in a crate or wood box.

Farm Dining Area

Our farmhouse is very small, about 1,000 square feet. It feels much larger because the living room, dining room, and kitchen are all one big room. To add elegance and comfort to our farm dining area, we went with upholstered French round-back chairs (Louis XVI).

A round gateleg table works perfectly in here. When purchasing a table, look at your space to see if it is more square or rectangular. A rectangular table often works best with a longer dining room, while a round or square table might work best for a square room. I changed out a square table for the round one because the square one allowed room for only four people. The round table can seat eight people comfortably when needed, but the sides can also be let down when seating is just needed for four or less. If you have a small space but need a larger table when guests come, try a drop leaf table, or a small table with leaves. The drop leaf tables will usually fit in a smaller space than a table with leaves.

Houston Heights House

This dining room is in a beautiful, new Craftsman-style home in the Houston Heights. Notice how the room doesn't have anything that matches. It's a collected look that feels like things were acquired over time.

The homeowner selected a modern version of a china cabinet that looks like a bookcase with doors. This type of china cabinet can really update a dining room space. It gives it a fresh look while still providing storage for china and silver.

The mirror in this room has a gorgeous patina. Mirrors are nice for dining rooms to reflect the light.

English Cottage

This home is new, but it was built in a traditional English cottage style. The beams keep with the English feel of the home, and yet they are quintessentially French at the same time. The banquette makes use of a small space and allows for flexible seating. The light streams into the room from the windows, and the grandfather clock gives the room grounding.

Soup tureens are great pieces to display because they are more three-dimensional than a plate. Vintage or new, they add warmth to a room.

China Cabinet Alternatives

If you take a close look at these rooms, not one of them contains a traditional china cabinet. One has a cabinet in the dining room, but it is more of a cupboard than a traditional china cabinet. If you want to give your dining room that designer look, I am going to suggest something you may find radical. Either get rid of your china cabinet or paint it. Now, this idea may be too "out there" for some, and if it doesn't appeal to you, then keep your china cabinet as is. Don't ever feel the need to implement someone else's ideas if you don't like them. This is something to consider if you want to do something totally different. You do not have to have a china cabinet in your dining room. It is not required by law, although some of us were raised to believe that. I don't have a china cabinet in my dining room. If you choose to not have a china cabinet, there are many other options.

What you can use instead of a china cabinet:

1. Open wood shelving

2. Wire wall shelf

3. Armoire

4. Console

5. Buffet

If you go with something shorter than a china cabinet, like a console (mine is about thirty inches tall), be sure to add a mirror or artwork above the console to add interest to the room. If you are unsure about getting rid of your china cabinet, try emptying it and moving it out of the dining room for a week to see if you like the look. If you are missing your china cabinet, it is still there, and you can put it back. If however, you decide you like the new openness of the dining room, you can now get rid of it with more confidence. I like to call this *reversibility*. Before I get rid of a piece, I move it out of the room to be sure I like the room without it. If I am undecided, I keep the old piece around for a week while I think about. Usually I know right away if I want to keep or get rid of something. Some people need more time to decide, and for them, a temporary move is best.

CHAPTER 14: THE LIVABLE LIVING ROOM

The living room (family room, den, great room, keeping room, or whatever you call it) is the room where you spend time with family and friends. This is where the family unwinds after a long day and where you entertain family and friends. Although I love an elegant look, the living room also needs to be practical and comfortable. I want comfy places to sit and visit and a cozy spot to curl up with a good book and a cup of tea. I want a seating arrangement that encourages talking. We live in a modern age, so most living rooms have a television. I know that needs to be factored in as well, but I don't want the TV to become what the room is about. The living room needs to be inviting.

I am a homebody. I sometimes hate to admit it, but it's true. I think that is why I enjoy feathering my nest so much. Home is where I want to be. It nourishes my soul. It welcomes friends, and it embraces my family. The living room is where much of that interaction happens.

Comfortable and Elegant

The living or family room is where the family spends time together, where they entertain friends, and where they live. Not to put too fine a point on it, but this is an important room. I like to accomplish two things with this room.

1. Give the room presence and elegance.

2. Make the room warm, welcoming, and comfortable.

I think a lot of people feel the need to decide whether the room will be comfortable or elegant. Why not both? It can be done! Sure, some beautiful chairs are not comfortable, but there are many comfortable chairs that are also elegant. I like to add a pretty, delicate chair in the room for form, but then make sure there is plenty of comfortable seating for people to actually use. The pretty chair is probably not the most comfortable chair in the room, so it likely won't get much use, but it still needs to be sturdy enough for someone to actually sit in it. If you do have a chair that isn't sturdy enough for seating, I recommend you put it in your bedroom where you are more certain someone won't actually use it. If, however, you do end up with a delicate chair in the living room, I highly suggest putting a stack of books or something else in the chair to discourage use.

Selecting furniture

I like to start with a full-sized comfy sofa. I feel strongly that every living room should have a sofa, unless one won't fit in the room. It needs to be big enough for taking a nap. That's my family's rule. Everyone in our family likes to nap, and there's always a race to see who gets to the sofa first at our house on Sunday afternoons. It's first come, first served.

I don't worry about the sofa being French. It needs to be comfortable, because it will probably be one of the most-used pieces of furniture in the room. Pick a silhouette that you like. There are so many choices: exposed legs or skirted sofas, high backs or low backs, big arms or low arms, three cushions or two cushions.

I really like sofas with slipcovers, because you can clean the slipcover if need be. A slipcover isn't necessary, but it's a nice bonus if it is available. Slipcovers also give you two potential looks for your sofa: with the slipcover and without. Sometimes you can buy new sofas with a slipcover. That would be ideal, because buying a custom-made slipcover can be expensive.

Slipcovers are typically washable, they extend the life of the sofa, and they can give a sofa with good bones a totally new look.

My sofa is a strong red color. Rather than throw it out when I changed to a neutral palette, I made custom slipcovers. It was much less expensive than buying a new sofa, but slipcovering requires advanced sewing skills. I used Italian linen for mine, but you could substitute drop cloth fabric if you were on a tight budget.

As for fabric, I prefer a solid color. Patterns come and go. Nothing will date your sofa faster than a strong pattern. Having worked in a furniture store, this is a lesson I learned early. A sofa with a solid color is going to stay in style much longer. Think wallpaper versus paint. As much as I love wallpaper, I have to admit it looks dated in a short time. And if you go with a patterned sofa, you will be much more limited as to what will go with the sofa fabric. If you are someone who loves patterns, add them with throws and pillows. Pillows are much cheaper to replace than sofas. The point is that a patterned sofa is not a mistake, but it is not as timeless as a sofa with a solid fabric, so it will probably end up costing you money in the long run.

If you are starting from scratch, I recommend selecting your sofa first. Then let that decision drive everything else. You can almost always find paint to coordinate with your sofa, but it isn't always easy to find a sofa you like that coordinates with your paint color. I prefer neutral fabric, but that may not be for you. If you want color, then go for the color. As I said, I recommend a solid color on the sofa. The sofa is one of your big-money purchases, and you want to stay happy with it as long as possible.

I have purchased two sofas with patterns that I quickly tired of and couldn't wait to replace. The patterns were strong and bold ones. I replaced them not because they were threadbare or worn but because I was tired of those patterns. If you prefer a patterned sofa, try a pattern that is classic and timeless.

After the sofa is selected, I like to add a French chair or two or three. The fastest way to make your room look French is to add one or more French chairs. Just keep in mind that the chairs need to be comfortable. You can always use large club chairs in the room for everyday use and just add a pretty French chair in the corner.

As for which chairs to put in the room, there are a lot of options for you to think about. I used French settees in my living room instead of chairs. I think they are quite comfortable but not as comfortable as a club chair would be. Just make sure your chairs are comfortable before you buy them.

I love the look of a delicate French chair. They are attractive and add a French feel. I love having at least one in each room.

There are lots of gorgeous choices for coffee tables, but most of the time I end up using an ottoman, since my feet end up there. Comfort is a factor, and an ottoman usually looks as good as a coffee table. When selecting an ottoman, look for one with pretty legs to add a layer of beauty to your room. That is a way to add style to the room without compromising comfort.

Not all of the wood furniture needs to match, but you don't want it to clash. For example, a red-based mahogany piece may not mix well with an antique pine piece. I avoid glossy mahogany and cherry woods in general. They seem more eighteenth-century English to me than

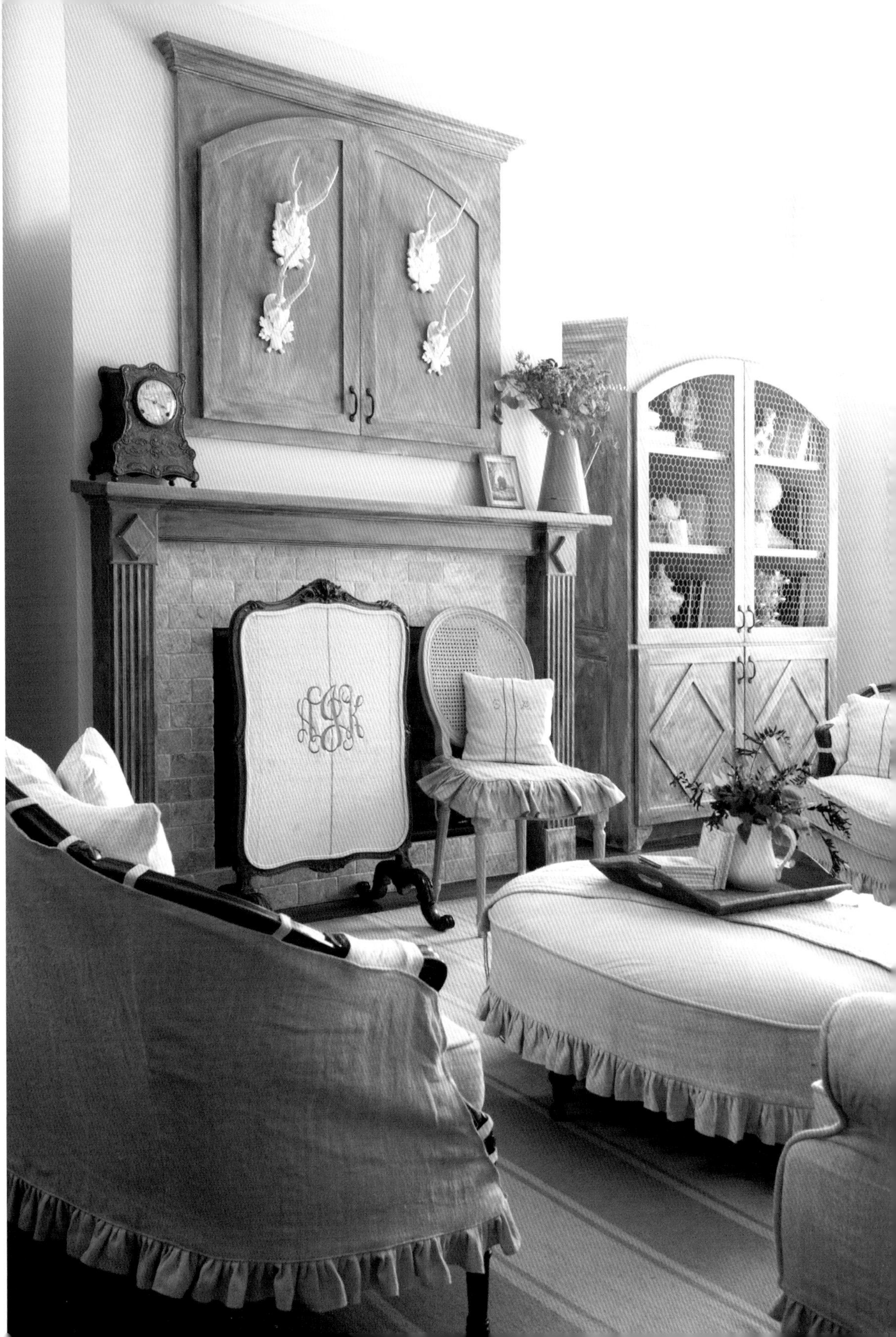

Slipcovered linen chairs and ottoman

French or farmhouse. I look for antique pine, walnut, and rustic, raw woods. A few years ago, my entire house was filled with in high-gloss mahogany. I mention it because I hear people say they are tired of mahogany but are stuck because their house is full of it. Even if you are on a tight budget, that may not be entirely true. Often, you can sell your old pieces on Craigslist and in consignment stores. With the money you make, you can buy used, inexpensive furniture.

If you love the bones of a piece but don't like the stain and finish, you can always paint it if you choose. I have painted my share of furniture, but I try to not overdo it. I don't want every piece of furniture in my home to be painted. I think balance is important. Painting is a fabulous solution; I just suggest that you don't paint everything.

I like to have at least a few pieces of French furniture in every room. It doesn't take much to give a room a French feel—just one or two pieces. I found a French table at an antique auction for twenty-five dollars. The top isn't in the best condition, but I think that just adds character; a perfectionist would run screaming from my house because most of my furniture is in less-than-perfect condition. My furniture is well loved and has some scratches and dents here and there. I don't worry about imperfections. If you buy vintage and antique furniture, it becomes increasingly difficult to find perfect furniture the older it is. Besides, once you get it home, the dog is going to bump into it or someone will kick it or drop something on it, so save yourself some grief and embrace the imperfections of furniture (and the imperfections of people in your life). In the long run, you'll be much happier.

Little tables are fairly easy to find at thrift and resale stores. I don't necessarily look for a French table, but rather a table with character. Antique and vintage tables are usually easy to find, reasonably priced, and have a lot more character than new ones.

Remember, if you aren't excited about something, *don't buy it*. Seriously. You will never like it, and you will either end up getting rid of it later or secretly wish you could get rid of it. It will be the piece you accidentally leave outside in the rain.

Furniture Arrangement

It is difficult to talk about how the furniture should be arranged in your room without seeing it. Still, there are a few rules of thumb I like to keep in mind. I like the room to be set up so that it looks its best from the direction you enter the room. Of course, you also need to make sure that the television can be seen from all chairs. The same goes for a fireplace. Depending on the size of the room and the amount of furniture in the room, you may have more than one seating area. Consider the traffic patterns, and make sure the room flows.

Here are a few suggestions:

1. Don't just push all of the furniture to the walls. Make sure chairs are close enough for those seated to have a conversation. If the room is large enough, break it up into two or more seating areas.

2. Try to arrange things so what you see as you enter the room is its best view. First impressions are as important for rooms as they are for people. I know you've heard it before, but you only

get one chance to make a good first impression. Make it count. This is the view that guests will most likely remember.

3. Try to remove extraneous furniture. Too much furniture makes the room feel cramped and uninviting. I know it's difficult, but you'll be glad you did.

4. For bedrooms, I like the bed to be on the opposite wall of the door if possible. I want to walk in and see the headboard from the door.

5. Buy some sliders and move the furniture around to try different arrangements.

6. Another helpful thing is to draw your room layout on grid paper and then make templates of all your furniture. Make sure your templates and the room are all to scale. I used this idea extensively before we moved. This worked for 90 percent of our furniture. Only a few pieces didn't work as planned.

Working with Built-ins

I've got mixed feelings about built-in furniture. It is great to have large bookcases or other built-in features since they are wonderful for storage and require less furniture to be purchased. If they are beautiful, then they can add drama and presence to the room. If they are unattractive, then you are pretty much stuck with them and sometimes end up trying to make them work when they just don't.

For built-ins to be an asset to a room, they need to be well designed. I wanted my built-in features to look custom, so I worked with the carpenter to ensure they looked more like furniture. Sometimes you get stuck with built-ins designed by someone else. So what do you do if they are uninteresting? You or your carpenter can add details to the cabinetry to make it more appealing. Trim can often be added or even removed. Depending on your budget, you could also have the built-in cabinets or shelves removed. One of my clients chose to remove built-in units that were in several rooms. The bedrooms looked so much better with the cabinetry removed, and now those bedrooms can be configured in many different ways. Before this change, furniture layout options were very limited. You can also alter cabinetry with paint. Look on Houzz.com and Pinterest.com to find ideas.

Styling Bookcases

There are many opinions on how to properly style a bookcase, and there are many ways to do it well. Here are my thoughts. Use vintage books. I know it sounds obvious, but people don't always put books in bookcases. One time, I filled mine with dishes. Did I say that out loud?

Sometimes to give the bookcase a uniform look, I turn the books backward so the spine faces the back of the bookcase. I like the look from a decorator standpoint, but you may not like this arrangement because you can't easily find a particular book in your bookcase. If it is a working library, then clearly this approach isn't going to work. If, however, the bookcase is filled with books that you rarely read, this look might be for you. Using the books turned backwards means they all have a uniform neutral white and creamy look. If the spines face out, then there will probably be types of colored book spines showing. That isn't as visually pleasing as just using one color palette.

Another tip I have for giving your bookcase a French feel is to add vintage items. They don't even have to be French. You can use old cameras, clocks, bookends, silver trophies, and bottles, just to name a few.

Styling a Fireplace

How you style a fireplace is important to the design of your home because the fireplace is often the main focal point for the room. And yet, I think it is one of the most difficult places to decorate because of limitations such as the mantel size and the size of the space above the mantel.

There are also heat issues, since there is potential for a roaring fire below. Many homeowners use this space for a flat-panel TV.

I prefer to not put the TV there, but often there is no other place for the TV, so it has to go above the fireplace.

When the television is above the fireplace, that means there are even more limitations to how you can decorate the space. Now you have to consider if something will block the view of the TV. If you have a TV above the mantel, the best thing to do might be not putting anything on the mantel. In my home, I had a cabinet built in the wall to house our TV. When the TV is not on, the doors are closed. Still, I can't put anything too tall on my mantel or it will get knocked over when the doors are opened. Putting something below or to the side of the television works better.

Why Go Neutral?

I love color. I mean, I *love* it. I have appreciated neutral homes for years in magazines and books, but I was one of the people that said I could never do that. I warmed to the idea gradually. At the end of the day, if you don't want to go neutral, then

don't! It's your house. For those of you that want to know my reasons for going neutral, here they are.

Neutral Is Always in Style

By definition, if something is a trend, it will be in style and then go out of style. Even many classic patterned fabrics look dated at some point. Neutral fabrics tend to stay in style for the long haul. Neutral in interior design is like the classic black dress. It's always in style.

Neutral Is Flexible

I have had three or four different sets of pillows I have used on my white linen sofa. When I had a strong pattern on my sofa, I couldn't find any pillows that would work, except the ones that came with the sofa. If you can't change out the pillows on a sofa, then you really are stuck with the same look every day, week, and month. People typically tire of a non-neutral sofa sooner than they do with a neutral one. If you like to change things often, this might be you. A white sofa has a lot more options for pillows than a sofa with color.

Neutral Is Less Expensive

This is something you probably won't hear anywhere else. I remember so many articles I have read over the years about decorators or designers who had a neutral home. They said they were bombarded by colors all day long, so they wanted soothing neutrals when they got home. Well maybe, but I suspect there is more to the story. The thing is, neutral is always in style. When you spend a lot of money on your furnishings (or even if you don't), you don't want to replace them every few years. For designers, decorators, and design bloggers, it's important that their homes are always in style. Since neutrals never really go out of style, you don't need to replace them very often. The savings comes from not having to replace neutral items. The items with color and patterns will look dated more quickly.

If you are thinking you want to change things up but you can't because your home is full of color, that is exactly what I thought. It was not easy for me to convert my home to neutrals, but I did it. I was able to keep costs down because I did all of my own sewing. It did require a good bit of my time, but I am *so* glad I did it. You pay one way or the other when you change your color scheme.

I love the soothing shades of white, cream, gray, and oatmeal in a neutral-colored home. If you have a neutral home or are considering going in that direction, I suggest that you not remove *all* color from the room. It may feel bland and flat with no color. Add a touch of color with some pillows, throws, a rug, artwork, flowers, or other accessories. I know after I spent months removing color from a room, it felt like I was going backward by putting color back in the room, but a bit of color is needed. The good news is that you can easily change the pillows or throws when you get bored with them. Better yet, if your whole house is neutral, simply move the accents around to different rooms for an entirely new look.

Neutrals are always in style, flexible, and less expensive in the long haul.

CHAPTER 15: BATHROOMS AND OTHER UTILITARIAN ROOMS

Bathrooms, also called *necessary rooms*, are often overlooked when decorating a house. These rooms are usually small, and people sometimes have a difficult time finding a way to make them feel special. When I was a kid, a well-decorated bathroom was one that had a matching toilet seat cover, U-shaped rug (around the toilet), and towels. If you had all of these, you had a very hip, modern, and "groovy" bathroom. Now things are different, and there are so many elegant, upscale bathrooms. You can't just slap a towel and a candle in your bathroom and call it "decorated" any more.

So how can you add style to a bathroom and give it some flair at the same time? Here are a few suggestions.

Easy Tips for Redoing Your Bathroom

Inexpensive Changes

1. Add a tub rack caddy to hold a book, soap, or washcloths.

2. Use a big jar to hold bath salts.

3. Use a vintage teacup as a scoop for bath salts.

4. Roll up towels and keep them in a basket or crate.

5. Keep a fresh stack of clean towels sitting out for use.

6. Store extra toilet paper in a basket, crate, or bucket.

7. Store electronics out of sight.

8. Fill a cup with dried lavender or potpourri.

9. Add decorative hooks for robes.

10. Set out a pretty dish of French soaps.

11. Set out pretty towels.

12. Change out the shower curtain for a new one.

Slightly Pricier Changes

1. Move a chair into the bathroom, if space permits.

2. Add a little table by the tub to hold a hand towel and soaps.

3. Use a small bookcase to hold towels.

4. Add a lamp.

5. Add an ottoman for extra seating.

6. Add a towel bar for wet towels.

7. Use a decorative, non-bathroom rug.

8. Replace the old-style frameless mirrors with new decorative ones.

9. Remove dated cabinet doors and replace with a curtain.

10. Cover the washer and dryer with a curtain.

If you are going to go to the expense of changing out light fixtures or plumbing fixtures, I highly suggest you go to a showroom, or at least check out an online site like Build.com. I have nothing against shopping at big builders' supply stores, but they will not have the selection that the online and specialty stores will have. I want you to see all of your options before you decide. Look online to see what options are available. After you have done your research, you can buy what you like with confidence.

It pays to do your research before you install anything in your home. Even if the item isn't expensive, if you have to pay a plumber or electrician to install or remove it, you want to minimize those labor charges. Make sure the item you have selected is the design you like best, but also do some checking to see what kind of reviews the product has. Just because an item is expensive doesn't mean it will be reliable and well made. Sometimes homeowners select expensive faucets or light fixtures that break in a short period of time. With online reviews available, it is easy to find out whether an item is recommended or not. Just remember, high price doesn't always translate into high quality.

Expensive Changes

1. Use furniture for storage instead of cabinets.

2. Add electrical outlets for hair dryers and toothbrushes inside cabinets.

3. Update faucets.

4. Update countertops.

5. Add a chandelier.

6. Update sinks.

7. Update lighting.

8. Add ceiling tiles to the bath ceiling.

Some people feel their bathrooms are too small to decorate, but that just isn't true. I agree that a small space means you will have fewer options, but there are many ways to spruce up the space. You can usually add attractive storage space on a wall with shelving or hooks. Outdated mirrors and lighting can usually be replaced.

City Bathroom

Our builder suggested we put a little coffee bar in our bathroom, since that is a popular accoutrement for new homes in our area. I told him to leave the space open instead so that we could put our armoire in the space. The armoire holds towels, washcloths, sheets, and even extra pillows. Why does it look so neat inside? I store only things inside that are the same color. Other colorful quilts and blankets go in the armoire in my bedroom. Things automatically look coordinated if they are all the same color, and that is why I organize towels and blankets by color.

Setting a chair and table by the tub is nice if you have room. The table can be used to hold towels and soaps, while the chair can be used when you are changing clothes.

It's so easy to add little accents without going overboard. This bath includes a vintage oyster basket full of rolled up luxury towels. A soft, welcoming robe sits on the chair at the ready.

On the other side of the bathroom, we used curvy mirrors to give the room a French feel. I found them at a discount store and then transformed them with paint and wax. The architectural prints on the wall showcase

Curvy French mirrors accent this white bath.

the buildings at Versailles. I chose not to use upper cabinets for a more open look. The light sconces also are very French in appearance.

The two tall pullout drawers house the hair dryers and toothbrushes. Our electrician set them up so that there is a power outlet in each drawer. Electric toothbrushes can be charged without being seen.

To give the room a spa-like feel, I added white plush robes to the room and hung them on some adorable little Scottie dog robe hooks. Since we are just talking about one or two hooks for robes, why not use a special hook rather than a plain one?

Girls' Bathroom

The bathroom down the hall is much smaller. Here I also used individual mirrors above each sink rather than one big mirror. The light fixtures have a curvy feminine feel to them that felt French to me. They may not be French, but if they are curvy, they will probably go with a French look. Because there was unused space between the mirrors, I added some artwork.

Downstairs Bath

This bath was lots of fun to design. I didn't want a traditional cabinet below the sink. I wanted something a bit more like furniture. I asked the carpenter to make the vanity like a little table. We used a marble bowl sink on top of the vanity and a wall faucet rather than the kind that connects to the vanity itself. The white granite on the vanity goes up the wall in an arched shape. I painted the vanity and distressed it using a technique similar to the one I covered in the chapter on painted furniture.

Underneath the vanity, we used an antique oyster basket from France to hold rolled white towels.

The wall sconce was meant to be used in a foyer, but I was able to fit it in above the mirror. The gray painted metal sconce has lots of French detail.

I used a wall anchor to attach the towel holder to the wall. The rest of the room was just as fun to plan. I added an antique gesso framed mirror to the wall above the claw-foot tub. Above the mirror sits a walnut pediment that became separated from an armoire long ago. I was attracted to the walnut wood, and all of the intricate carving on the pediment. For a cornice board over the tub, I used a piece of salvaged barn wood.

For a towel holder, I didn't want anything ho-hum. I found an old wooden finial and used it to hold the hand towel.

It is worn in a way that you just can't replicate with new wood. Then I added the lace panels. Since this tub isn't currently being used, lace panels worked fine. If you want to use lace panels, or any other drapes as a shower curtain, be sure to add a shower curtain liner to keep the water inside the tub.

This little bath is more contemporary with its tilt mirror and quartizite countertop. The light fixture and the towel rack add a more flea market feel to the room.

Country Guest Cottage Bath

This bathroom shown on the right is rustic. It certainly isn't considered traditional French style. When people think French, they think elegant, refined, and upscale. But I love to see French touches in all types of decor and find that it is just as much at home with rustic farmhouse style as it is with high-end contemporary design. I love the mix of rustic with refined. It reminds me of *Green Acres*, and really, Lisa Douglas was the one who originally came up with the shabby but elegant look. At the end of the day, the rest of us are just copying her style.

This room feels very "farmhouse" to me. The artwork, the chandelier, and the curved mirror could be considered French. It is not a traditional French look, as I said. I love mixing rustic farmhouse touches with elegant French style.

Luxury Farm Bath

The next bathroom is so fun and also has a hint of French. The silver, the wire shelf, and the marble are some excellent elements, but my favorite is the

mannequin head. Of course she is wearing a tiara!

This owner chose to leave her windows uncovered, a bold move for a bathroom. It opened up the view to the outdoors. The wire shelf, the silver, the tiara, and the claw-foot tub add so many layers of details.

Grace Meadows Bathroom

The soft blue of this bathroom is so refreshing. I love the way the light floods the room. A clawfoot tub completes the look. The little cabinet between the sinks holds towels and a mirror.

Round Top Guest Bath

Using a more rustic approach, this bath incorporates an old sliding barn door at the entrance

to the room. Inside, the shiplap walls add charm to the bathroom. Using a vintage mirror and wall cabinet also adds so much interest and texture to the room.

The antique tin tiles on the ceiling complete the look. This room has so much to love from the floor all the way to the ceiling, and the truth is, it is a small bathroom. This goes to show you can pack a lot of charm and detail into a small space!

Marble countertops make for a soft, pretty look.

Round Top Master Bath

Another rustic bath, shown on the right, has a bead board ceiling and shiplap walls. The open cabinet stores bath supplies and towels. The small French table provides a place for towels or toiletries, while the chair is a great place to sit while changing clothes or putting on shoes.

English Cottage Baths

The double-sided slipper tub fits snugly in a small bathroom packed with charm. The stone wall and beams give it a cottage feel. I like the brick floor and stone wall. It's a nice departure from an all-white bathroom.

Elegant Master Bath

This amazing bathroom reminds me of a ship's cabinetry. The arched top is stunning. The marble wall behind the mirrors adds beautiful detail to the room. A tub sits opposite the vanity, with lots of detailed cabinetry and stylish windows.

Closets

If you have a small closet, like I had for most of my life, then there aren't a lot of things you can do to decorate it, but there are a few things you can do to make it the best it can be.

1. Color-code your clothes.

Not only does this make your closet look neater, but it also makes it a whole lot easier to find what you are looking for. I also organized my clothes by long-sleeve shirts, short-sleeve shirts, shorts, pants, and dresses. This organization makes it even easier to find what I am looking for.

2. Use storage boxes for organization.

Another thing you can do is use pretty boxes or baskets to organize and corral small objects in the closet.

3. Pick up clutter off the floor.

4. Add a chair or table if room allows.

5. Get rid of clothes you don't actually wear.

Even though my current closet is large, I didn't want it to become a junk shop. Rather than store stuff in there that I was never going to use again, I started giving things away that I wasn't wearing.

Since we had the home custom built, I got to work with the carpenter to design a wall of built-in drawers and cabinets. We keep sweaters, socks, and sheets in the drawers. With such a large closet, I wanted to make use of the space in the center of the closet. I had never had so much room in a closet before. Rather than go with a built-in island, I decided to keep the middle of the closet open. If I put an island in the center of the room, then I would be stuck with it later, even if I changed my mind. Using furniture instead, I can always completely redo the room if I so choose. I still have the option of moving a chest in there if I decide I need more storage. Now there is a desk and two chairs, but tomorrow, I could move that all out and put a simple, large ottoman in the center. It is much more flexible if you don't go with too many built-ins. I work with clients who are stumped by big built-in cabinets that have been installed in bedrooms. We usually rip them out. Few built-ins look as good as real furniture.

With the open space in my closet, I decided to create a little French hideaway. I started with gray paint on the built-ins. Then I used an elegant chandelier in the center of the closet. If we are barely awake and don't want a lot of light, we turn on the chandelier, which is fitted with twenty-five-watt bulbs. If we need more light for checking color matches, we turn on the canned lights. All of the lights come on if we are trying to determine if a sock is navy or black.

In the center of the closet, I added a French table and two leather Louis XV chairs. I know this closet is a real luxury, and to have room for a table and two chairs is beyond what I ever thought we would have. To be honest, it's a bit tight, but I really like having the seating area. Even if your closet isn't this big, my hope is that you can discover some ideas for use in your space.

Laundry Room

Laundry rooms are also notoriously small, but still there is room to make them charming with some French accents. I added a candle chandelier to the ceiling. It is nonelectric, and the beauty of the candle version is that you can put them about anywhere, because they don't require electricity. Rather than plastic laundry baskets, use wicker for a country French feel.

CHAPTER 16: DREAMY BEDROOMS

Making a Bedroom Cozy

Bedrooms are meant to be a place to recharge. They should be beautiful and cozy, a place that surrounds you with warmth and comfort. The bedroom is not only where you sleep but also where you want to enjoy quiet and rest. The room should embrace, not shock, so I don't like jarring things in the bedroom. Instead, I prefer soft, natural fabrics and soothing vistas.

For my own room, I chose a soft, neutral, and relaxing palette. When using muted colors in the room, it's important to include lots of textures and a hint of color. This bedroom includes texture from the bed linens, artwork, bamboo shades, wood light sconces, reclaimed hardwood floor, and furniture.

Since the bed takes center stage, it's critical that you love it. You will likely be spending a good bit of time there. Be sure to select bedding that is soft and inviting. I had previously spent a small fortune on gorgeous red bedding that, although beautiful, didn't work with my new neutral palette. I had to think long and hard about no longer using that bedding, since it was so expensive. In the end, I decided to keep it . . . in the closet . . . where no one could see it. If I ever want to use it again, the bedding is there, but in the meantime, it's not holding me hostage to a red room.

The finance industry would call the red bedding a sunk cost. The cost was in the past, and there is no way you can get that money back. But that doesn't mean I can't change out the bedding. And I could sell the old bedding if I wanted to.

After deciding to move away from the red, I then searched for the bedding of my dreams. I couldn't find exactly was I was looking for, so I decided to sew it myself from oatmeal-colored Italian linen. Since my settee and ottoman were also red, I knew I would have to make slipcovers for them as well. Making the slipcovers was much less expensive than having them reupholstered, and it is completely reversible, should I ever decide to go back to the original red upholstery.

The duvet at the foot of the bed is an antique French bedspread carefully gathered around a feather duvet. I bought the delicate antique bedspread with a plan to convert it to a duvet cover, but as often happens with antique materials, I found I couldn't take a scissor to this antique French work of art.

The antique French pine armoire is topped with an equally old French laundry basket. Like many treasures, this large basket was found at the Round Top Antique Show. The

basket adds texture and authenticity to the room.

The armoire, filled to the brim with stacks and stacks of family quilts and linens, reminds me of my grandmother's house. On cold evenings, we wrap ourselves in layer upon layer of quilts, made by aunts and grandmas.

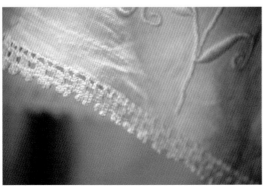

I love adding vintage touches to a room, and family heirlooms hold special value to me. It was so much fun to display the wedding gown my mother-in-law wore on a warm Virginia day in 1946. Hung over the top of our old armoire, this satin and tulle wedding gown looks like the bride could be popping in at any minute to finish preparations

for her special day. Displaying family treasures like this inherited family wedding dress makes the space personal and meaningful to the owner. I loved the look so much that I added my own wedding gown to the mix.

I really appreciate the warm, weathered pine in this antique French armoire. New pine pieces simply don't have the patina you see in antique pine pieces.

A great way to add interest to a room is to use things in a new or unusual way. The cabinet I use as a side table was once the top of a grandfather clock. Adding the shelf inside meant I could display an assortment of antique and vintage dishes inside the cabinet.

When designing a room, I like to think outside of the box. I want to not only create something beautiful but also something unique. When I converted a mirrored armoire in another room to a china cupboard, I had to remove the wood panel behind the mirrored glass. That wood armoire door panel sat in my guest room for years, waiting for just the right project. When I decided to hang a candle sconce

in my bedroom, the idea emerged to use the old armoire door as a base for the candle sconce. The door acts as a frame for the sconce, giving it more presence in the room and adding an additional element of surprise and a "wow" factor.

To create an authentic French feel to a room, I used objects with lots of age. Sometimes the patina is from a hundred years of wear, and sometimes it is simply a faux finish used on the piece. The chipped paint finish on the settee and the stacked tables is the real deal. The settee is quite old. I left the worn tapestry fabric because I really liked it. I felt new fabric would have taken away from the charm of the settee. The chipping paint also provides an authentic feel that might have been lost had I covered it with a coat of fresh paint. I love the elegant shabbiness of the threadbare tapestry.

Using pieces that show their age adds depth and appeal to a room. Using only pristine, brand-new pieces can make a room feel stuffy and too perfect.

Although new, the sconces and lamps in the room appear to have an aged patina. I like to use a mix of new items along with antiques in the same room.

Linen is one of my favorite fabrics to use when creating bedspreads or slip-covers. Some people are put off by the abundances of wrinkles, but the wrinkles tell me the fabric is real linen. Nothing hangs quite like linen, and ruffles made in other fabrics just don't look like the same. It launders well, and because it is cool to the touch, linen is perfect for our hot, Texas climate.

When I found a French vanity at a nearby thrift store, it certainly didn't look like much. It was stained an unattractive orange-brown, and the bench was topped in a tattered, worn, rusty-red velvet fabric. Since the fabric color was not going to work with the other fabrics in my room, I opted to replace it with a simple French blue-striped linen. I also painted the vanity gray and distressed it to go with the antiques in the room.

The mirror over the vanity is a French Louis Felippe from before 1870. It was partially painted black when I bought it. I knew the black paint was not original, and it upset me greatly to see the mirror painted in that garish morbid fashion. I painted over the black straight away because I couldn't stand it.

Later, when we traveled to Paris, I told my host, Madame Catherine, about how horrified I was to find my mirror painted black. She said that when Napoleon III lost the war in 1870, he lost part of France. The French people were so upset that they went into mourning. To show their

collective grief, they painted much of their furniture and accessories black. That was an eye-opener. Lesson learned. Don't assume you know everything. (I'm talking to myself here!) I'm still not sorry I painted it, despite the fact that I painted over paint that had been added in 1870.

Evangeline's Room

Toile (pronounced *twäl*) is one of my favorite fabrics. It says "French" like nothing else. This bedding was made in the same fashion as the bedding on my bed. Placing a quilt or duvet at the foot of the bed makes it even more inviting, even if the weather is warm.

An easy way to add architectural interest to a room is to add louvered doors behind the bed. I painted the doors and then distressed them using an antiquing glaze. An antique mirror hangs in the center of the doors to give the room a bit of drama and a focal point. If you use shutters or louvered doors behind your bed, you could easily eliminate the need for a headboard, but I already had one for the bed.

The large basket at the foot of the bed holds the bedding when my daughter sleeps at night. The big basket was found at a discount store, but with its leather straps, you would never guess what a bargain it was.

I am particularly fond of French demilune tables, but they can be pricey and hard to find. The demilune tables in this room were found at a discount store, but the color of the tables didn't match. One was black and the other one was covered in a cherry stain. A coat of gray paint made the set look matched.

Elise's Room

I love the rusty antique iron bed in this room. I found it at a thrift store for next to nothing. It had just come into the store, and it left immediately in my car. The bed, although not actually French, reminds me of simple country French decor.

My daughter enjoys sharing a snack with a friend while seated at the little table. From this upstairs bedroom, they can savor tea and scones as they watch birds playing in the pear tree beyond the window. A basket at the end of the bed holds blankets and an extra pillow, should they be needed in the night.

A large mirror placed above the bed becomes the clear focal point in this room. A decorating mistake I see often is using undersized artwork above a bed.

A room, much like a movie, tells a story and has a leading actor or actress. For bedrooms, the bed is the lead, and what that lead wears needs to be consistent with the storyline. The storyline for a room is the feeling you want to create. I wanted this bedroom to feel fun and fresh, while maintaining a rustic French charm. I pictured a simple yet elegant bed much like you would find in the book *Madeline* by Ludwig Bemelmans. This white bedding appears simple, yet it is trimmed in beautiful lace.

Not surprisingly, I couldn't find what I wanted in the stores. I turned to my own linen closet for the answer. I found an unused daybed skirt that created the exact look I wanted. If you decide to use a bed skirt as a bedspread, keep in mind that many of the inexpensive versions don't have a pretty top. To find one of this quality will probably cost as much or more than a nice bedspread.

I made a simple, easy bulletin board from an unused frame and chicken wire so we could display some family photos and mementos in this room. I've attached old hymnals and vintage family photos to personalize the space. The lamps purchased originally for another room work in here, because the rusty lamps echo the rusty finish of the iron headboard.

Using a gray and white paint combination on the armoire gave it an updated and elegant look. It hides a TV when it isn't in use. Whenever possible, I like to hide the TV and electronics from view.

I always tell people I like rusty, crusty, and chippy things. The bed suits me to a rusty T. The rust finish on the bed frame made my heart beat just a little bit faster. So the rust wouldn't ruin clothing or the delicate white bedding, I used a clear sealer all over the bed frame.

Although a bit unconventional, throughout the house I used a darker gray on all the doors. The doors become works of art, and they really stand out. The mahogany doors were custom made with French arches, pieced together the old-fashioned way. I used new crystal doorknobs in

keeping with the old-world feel of the home. If you decide on antique doorknobs, remember that it's difficult to find enough matching hardware for an entire house. One option is to just use an antique doorknob on a feature door, like a pantry.

In the city, I took a slightly more formal approach to French design. At the farm, I wanted a look compatible with relaxation and ease. The farmhouse is our getaway from a somewhat harried city life, so it was important that things remain casual and able to stand up to heavier wear and tear.

The Three Little Bears' Room

This is a room at the farm where both of my girls sleep, with an extra bed thrown in for a friend, since we often have guests at the farm. In keeping with the simplicity of the farm setting, I used gingham lavender duvets on each bed.

Each bed has its own basket for personal items and an ottoman that I slipcovered in burlap. With only one dresser in the room, it was important to include extra places for storage.

The dresses on the walls are family pieces. One of the dresses was worn by both of my girls. Another dress was purchased by my mother-in-law while she was expecting her first baby. Since that baby was a boy, and there never was a daughter, the dress was never worn, which explains its pristine condition. I love using the iron display frames because I can take down the dresses if we ever tire of them and hang something else on the wire frames instead. Without these iron pieces, the small dresses would get lost on the large wall.

The single French dresser in the room looks right at home with the green French mirror.

Cedar Hill Farm Bedroom

This next bedroom is my happy place at our farm. The painting features my husband's family farmhouse before it was destroyed by fire.

Here I wanted something very simple and neutral, yet brimming with French charm. Blue-striped French ticking seemed to be the perfect solution. The ticking is humble and simple, fitting for a farm. Although I would classify the

duvet cover as neutral, the blue stripe gives the room a French feel while adding just a hint of color. The casual fabric works beautifully with the other simple furnishings in the room.

Simple leggy French chests on either side provide much needed storage in this small house, while the oyster baskets neatly store magazines.

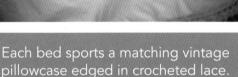

Each bed sports a matching vintage pillowcase edged in crocheted lace.

Being a Southerner, I am required to have at least one monogram in my house. It's in the handbook, after all. So I added a monogrammed pillow to this bed. The old blue bottles were some special finds from Round Top, while the white iron-stone pitcher, holding lavender roses, is a family heirloom.

On the other side of the room sits an antique farm desk with a dreamy view down to the pasture. It's a great place to work, where I can look out the window and day-dream when I should really be working. The farm table is old, from the nineteenth century. The antique French mirror is full of character with the leaf and berry design.

Did I mention I love toile? Yes, I think I did. I added it to the back of my French linen press and to the inside of the doors. Adding fabric to the inside of furniture is an easy way to add some character to a piece of furniture. With this type of detail, it's tempting to leave the doors open all day long.

Guest Quarters

This is where guests stay at our house. The bedding is a mishmash of things. The cover is actually a bed skirt. The duvet at the foot of the bed is covered in a vintage tablecloth. The crocheted throw on the bench is also a vintage tablecloth. The euro shams were vintage shams that had never been used, possibly left in a hope chest. I used a column table as a nightstand to give the room an aged look. A large bottle on the column is used as a hat stand.

Vintage grain sacks are displayed on the vintage ladder. An extra handmade quilt sits in the olive bucket for those cold nights.

Angling the bed in the corner gave it more drama and presence. To give it just the right amount of romance, I converted a canned light in the space so we could install a chandelier there. The large artwork hides a secret. The television sits behind it. When guests want to watch their favorite show, they need only move the lightweight canvas off the cabinet. The cabinet hides my sewing machine and sewing notions.

Texas Farmhouse Bedrooms

This blue and white bedroom is full of peace and calm, yet it still has lots of charm. The original oil painting above the bed, painted by a local artist, adds a pop of color and interest to the wall above the bed. The crisp white and blue bedding feels inviting against the backdrop of the blue walls.

The basket at the foot of the bed holds extra sheets and blankets.

The farmhouse guest room to the left boasts two twin beds right under an upstairs window. This window looks out over the pasture where the horses graze. The soft blue and white embroidery on the bedding has a gentle beauty. Grandchildren make use of the room when they visit from the city.

Sear's Kit House Bedroom

This next room has a lovely vaulted ceiling with a round window above the bed. The floor is covered with a large gorgeous Aubusson rug. The house was actually originally a made from a Sears kit. Here you can see out the windows onto a pool and creek. The owner has many collections and a great eye for details. I could spend all day at her house and still find something new to see the next day.

You might think that is all you can fit in the room, but if you thought that, you would be wrong.

I love this gorgeous lamp and the medical-type head statue. In another part of the bedroom sits this Victorian entry hall piece with some of the owner's amazing collections.

A chandelier hangs down next to the bed for some bling and light.

Pool House

This home has the most amazing pool house. I have heard people say that city folk may collect cars, but country folk collect houses. There's a bit of truth in that. With the overhead doors open, the pool house becomes an open-air kitchen and place to visit next to the pool. With the doors down, it's a little studio guest cottage with a charming kitchen, bath, and sleeping area.

The two daybeds can be used for seating or for sleeping. The concrete floor means there is no worry about hardwood scratches or spills on carpet.

The owner's creativity is amazing! She used a basket around a chandelier in the corner, and the walls are made from salvaged shiplap.

She has a vintage fan in the cottage, which comes in handy on hot summer days.

I love the old stack of books and the antique bust.

English Cottage Bedrooms

The stone walls in the cottage are the first things you notice. Although in Texas, this cottage was built to look like it could stand in the English Cotswolds. English-style works beautifully with French details, so this home is full of French touches. The mirror in the bedroom is curvy and beautiful. The dresser also has lots curves.

The Swedish headboards are charming with the two twin beds. Creamy matelassé bedding adds a flirty detail to the room.

The second bedroom at the English cottage also has stone walls, which help insulate the home from the heat during the summer. Linen bedding adds a feeling of luxury to the room.

The bed is topped with vintage lace netting for a gorgeous effect.

A bedroom should be relaxing and provide a soft place to fall. While each bedroom highlighted here is different, they all share a common theme; they all have a touch of French flare while providing a cozy place to refresh and renew. A bedroom is the last place you see before you go to sleep and the first place you see when you wake up. Shouldn't it be a special place that embraces you?

Round Top Blue Room

This room, tucked in the back of the house, has character to spare. The rustic fence acts as a headboard behind one of the beds. A mirror adds French flair to the room in an understated way. The blue toile quilts are just as charming as can be, paired with the long burlap bed skirts. Shiplap walls and bamboo window shades add texture to the room.

Rustic Bedroom

This bed uses a reclaimed shelf as a headboard. Above the shelf sits a long mirror perfect for the space. The crown candle sconces provide the perfect touch of bling to the room. Mismatched lamps work beautifully on either side of the bed, since they both hold their own. The burlap bench provides a nice place to sit while getting dressed in the morning.

Country Guest Cottage

This adorable guest cottage provides so much charm, guests will have a hard time leaving. A bookcase has a wonderful collection of vintage items. A converted crib acts as a settee in the room. Soft lavender duvets cover each of the twin beds that flank a small French hutch. The mirror is another French beauty.

CHAPTER 17: OUTDOOR LIVING

Making Outdoor Spaces Inviting

Our house sits in the middle of neighborhood founded in the late 1800s. At that time, with no air-conditioning, people spent a lot of time outdoors enjoying a cool breeze or any air movement they could catch in the summer. Porches were a vital part of the home. This was the time when a porch was used for sleeping in the summer, because bedrooms were often too hot. Neighbors spent a good bit of time on their porches, not only trying to find respite from the oppressive heat but also as a form of socializing.

Before computers, TV, and social media, the way most people communicated was in person, and that was what the front porch was for—visiting. A visitor would be offered a seat and a cold glass of iced tea. Neighbors might be strolling by, and they would be hailed and often invited over for a visit. This is the atmosphere I like to re-create on my porches. I love that neighbors are constantly walking by my house.

One of the biggest tips I can give about making outdoor rooms livable is to treat them, as much as possible, like an indoor space and decorate them like you would an indoor space. Of course, you'll need to make some adjustments for the elements, which I'll discuss in the next section.

So what can you do to make your porch, deck, patio, or other outdoor area inviting?

Try to include the following:

1. Comfortable seating (Obviously, the bigger the porch, the more seating you will be able to provide.)

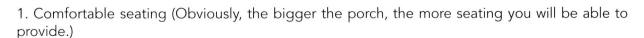

2. Pillows

3. Blankets, quilts, and throws in cooler weather

4. Side tables (If you have room.)

5. Dining table (If you have room.)

6. Indoor and outdoor rug

7. Rockers

8. A porch swing

I even have two daybeds outdoors. Stuffed with lots of pillows, they work beautifully as sofas, but remove the pillows and you have a comfortable place to take a nap and feel the breeze. I just love having as many places as possible to sit and visit with friends and family.

Protection from the Elements

There is a secret to keeping indoor fabrics nice when they are in use on an outdoor porch. You don't want them to get wet or get too much exposure to the sun. Critters can also be an issue. My advice is to bring in the pillows and seat cushions when not in use. I know this is not what you want to hear, but it's true. I've tried leaving cushions

and pillows outdoors at the farm. The fabrics were outdoor fabrics made to stand up to the elements, but the mice destroyed them. Candles left outdoors were dragged behind furniture and gnawed—mercilessly. But that's at the farm. The cushions at my city house fare much better. I don't have a problem with mice in the city, but the squirrels have really torn up some cushions on my front porch. Then there's the cat who thinks our front porch is his, but otherwise he's pretty harmless.

The bedding on my back porch and at our tree house go indoors at night. So far, almost everything has survived. I've had one table get ruined when it got too wet, but everything else has done well. The other thing I do is tarp my wood tables when the weather is foul, or when we aren't there. I paint the iron furniture once a year. Keeping things outdoors means they will require a lot more maintenance.

I recommend checking what the manufacturer suggests, although I have dragged a china cabinet, daybed, and a few tables onto my porch that were meant for indoor use only. Things get dirty in the country, so I am also always wiping things down. It's a lot of work. But having said that, I feel it is well worth the effort.

Idyllic Outdoor Dining

When I think of French dining, my thoughts go to our experiences dining at outdoor tables along sidewalks in Paris. These trips to France were halcyon days. Having read many a decor magazine (like a teenager eagerly soaking up a gossip magazine), I had read about many a family meal at a long table beside an old stone country home in the south of France. The wood table, having been pulled out of the house earlier that day along with odd chairs, would be set up elegantly using family linens, country crockery, and real silverware. There were no plastic sporks to be found and no processed foods, paper plates, or paper napkins. These affairs were considered rustic by French standards but were still incredibly

elegant. That is the look I strive for—a look that says, "Welcome, I'm glad you are here!" I want my guests to know they are special and that I went to a little extra effort to make our meal an event.

I don't use my best china outdoors, but I do use real dishes. When taking a picnic basket to our creekside deck, I often grab some enamelware plates and mugs, so I don't have to worry about breakage.

My family loves taking a meal outdoors. Even a cup of tea or coffee is so much more delightful when enjoyed on the back porch.

My Back Porch

The daybed sitting on our back porch makes the space so inviting. People don't often put a bed on the porch these days, but before air-conditioning, it was not unusual for families to sleep on the porch. I love taking a nap out here.

My favorite place to enjoy a meal with friends is at the long antique scrubbed pine farm table on our back porch. From the table, you can see hay bales, trees down the hill, and the sun setting in the evening. The china cabinet is next to the table on my back porch. Well, why not?

Bev's Porch

My friend Bev has an amazing home with lots of fabulous porches, so she could quite easily live on her porch if she had to. Here, she used an antique baby buggy frame and added a board to create a unique coffee table.

Having a wonderful table on the porch means you can dine in style outside. It's like a picnic but with more comfortable seating and closer to a stove and refrigerator. It also means you can use real dishes.

I love using real dishes outdoors. Yes, every time you use a plate, you run the risk of breaking it, but what is the point of having something that doesn't get used?

I just don't think you can have too many places to sit outdoors. When you have company, you can spread out and use several different seating areas.

Round Top

The cupola adds a vintage feel to the outdoors. Although not French, the cupola *feels* French with the curves, and I love the rusty metal. That gives it lots and lots of appeal.

English Cottage Garden

Dinner for two at an iron bistro table in a manicured courtyard is so very French in my book. This enchanted garden makes for a luxurious place to linger over a meal.

The Fields

Even without a porch, it's simple to have an outdoor meal. You can easily set up a folding table or even bring a table outside for an impromptu meal. Everything tastes better outdoors anyway. Granddad always said that,

The head vase is an original. These vases were quite popular in the thirties and forties. I remember my grandma had one.

and he was right. I've been known to carry chairs and a table out to the fields or even into the woods for a special meal. You can also haul a bed outside. (Yes, I've done that too.) But if that's too much work, a hammock might be just the thing for you.

Molly, our farm collie, loves to frolic in the wildflowers.

Adirondack rocking chairs make the back porch a destination.

Tiny Chapel

This charming little chapel is a real favorite of mine. It is so lovely and very much in keeping with my farmhouse French theme, so I had to include it in my book. I knew about the chapel long before I met Leslie, its charming owner. Taking our little all-terrain vehicle around the nearby dirt roads, we happened upon this chapel one day. I wanted to know more about it. It had country charm; I knew there was a story there.

About a year later, when volunteering at our local church, I met the owner! Leslie, a delightful soul, had the chapel built before they even had a house on the property. It is built in a style similar to the way churches were built in this area when it was originally settled in the early 1800s.

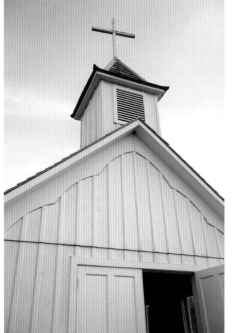

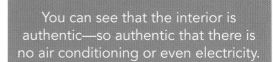

You can see that the interior is authentic—so authentic that there is no air conditioning or even electricity.

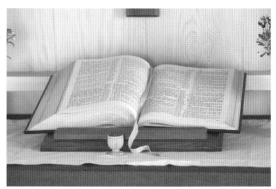

Little Gray House

Cecile's home is amazing, and her outdoor spaces are some of the best places to sit outside and enjoy the views. She has a side porch where we can see the sunset.

The front of the house provides yet another spot to sit a spell, with chairs, a bench, and even a porch swing.

Catch a breeze on the quaint front porch.

CHAPTER 18: BEFORE AND AFTER

It's one thing to show pictures of a decorated room, but how do you do it? What is the thought process? How do you decide what to keep, what get rid of, and what to buy? Let me share with you my creative process. Here I'll show you my process start to finish: the decisions I made and the end result.

Before and After Blue Bedroom

Here is the process I went through to transform my farmhouse bedroom from cottage style to Farmhouse French style.

From looking at the photos and my own tour of the room, I made some quick notes about it:

- Paint: Although I would prefer a gray color on the walls, the current color is quite nice (Sherwin-Williams Windsor Greige), so I won't repaint the room. I would prefer a shade more toward gray, but since the color is fine, this is an expense that isn't worth it for me. I suspect a lot of people have to work with a paint color they selected years ago.

Before Photos

- Bedding: Although I still like the green bedding, I wanted to go with blue.
- Rug: Although it went with the original green bedspread, I am no longer using that bedspread, and this rug does not have a French feel, and it is the wrong color. It needs to go! Replace with neutral rug.
- The painting is not the look I am going for in this room.
- Lamps on nightstands are not working.
- Nightstands: keep.
- Wicker chair looks too casual and the other chair doesn't look comfortable; they have to go.
- Stacked footstools between chairs: Cute but not elegant enough for this room. Move them out.
- Chair at the desk: I don't like it for this room.
- The painting above the desk is green and yellow and is not going to work well with my new blue and white room.
- Green ladder on wall: This might be too casual. I may need to move that depending on what I do here.
- French linen press works great; leave it.
- Antique desk is great; leave it.

Now I can make a list of things I need for the room:

1. Neutral rug

2. Two comfy French chairs

3. Little side table to go between the two French chairs

4. Two new lamps for the nightstands

5. New bedding

6. New artwork above the bed

7. New artwork above the desk

8. New desk chair

Some rooms need just a few things; I would call this a pretty substantial list of things to replace. If you are working on a budget, it may take months to replace everything or maybe just a few days if you can move items in from another room. Not everything has to be bought at once. Now I have a starting point.

For this room, I now have a buying list. I'll tell you how I selected new items and where I bought them. I'm also listing the items in order so you can see which purchases triggered other changes.

Bedding

When I decorate a bedroom, it is difficult to find bedding that is just right for the room, so I like to select the bedding before I select any other fabrics for the room.

This gorgeous French blue ticking duvet and pillows came courtesy of Ballard Designs. I chose this bedding because it is simple and casual, yet elegant and full of style. The blue stripe gives it a French feel, so I felt

Before and after purchase #1:
Blue bedding and a smaller, more neutral rug

like this was the perfect bedding for my room. I was also in the mood for blue, but in a small dose, so the narrow blue stripe was perfect. Although a bed skirt is not necessary with this bed frame, I felt that a bed skirt added some softness and romance to the room. When I couldn't find a bed skirt in linen the correct length for this bed, I made my own.

Neutral Rug

I knew I wanted a neutral rug. I was looking at some sisal rugs and also some wool rugs. I ended up getting this simple rug at Target. Be careful buying rugs over the Internet; colors are often not true, and you can't examine the fiber in person. Not all rugs are of equal quality. It is much smaller than the first one, but I think it works in the room.

Pair of Comfy French Chairs

Before and after purchase #2:
Chairs upholstered in grain sack fabric

People ask me all the time where I get my chairs and why I choose the ones I do. As for these chairs, it was all dependent on what was available at my resale shops within my budget. I never know what is going to be available because it is all secondhand. What is in the store one day will be quite different from what is available another day in another month. I wanted two nice French chairs in the room, but I knew better than to say they have very strict requirements because I didn't know what would become available at my favorite shops. As is often the case, providence stepped in. I just happened to be at Alabama Furniture in Houston, consigning some of my old furniture, and I saw two chairs covered in rust-colored fabric.

What the chairs looked like when I got them.

They looked pretty bad. In fact, someone had already started pulling the old fabric off the chairs but didn't finish. I bought them right away since they were a decent price. I don't have a lot of room for chairs in this space, but these bergère chairs are small, and I knew they would work perfectly. I had them re-covered in vintage grain sack fabric for the backs and a matching oatmeal-colored linen for the seats. Even when you consider my total cost (the chairs + fabric + labor), they were about half of what I would've paid for them had I found them already re-covered in linen and grain sack fabric. For the best deals, you will need to go often to your favorite resale shops and check the stock. If they get what you want in the store, you need to move quickly and buy it before someone else does. Don't stop to think about it too long or wait for the price to go down. Finding new chairs was certainly an option, but they would not have all of the marvelous hand carving like these chairs do. When looking at old chairs like these, make sure to factor in the cost of fabric and the upholstery labor. It is not always cheaper to buy vintage and re-cover. I went with vintage chairs not to save money but because I wanted those beautiful carved details.

Had these chairs not been available, I would have considered some other options. I could have used only one chair if necessary, but I did hope for a matching pair. I chose the grain sack and linen fabric because they are fabrics I love to work with, and I already had them in my workroom. I also knew the grainsack stripe would be fabulous with my new blue bedding.

Little Side Table

I knew that the chairs I was adding were much more upscale than the old chairs. The stacked step stools I had used in my previous bedroom design were not going to work with my new chairs. I also needed something small for my space. I didn't want a table that was too tall, because I thought it would look odd next to the chairs. I thought of using a round side table, but the tall ones looked like plant stands. It needed to be the correct height for my chairs. Since I shop at secondhand stores, I never know what stock will be available on any given day.

Purchase #3: Small side table

I looked at new tables and old tables. I wanted something unique, but again, it had to be small. That eliminated most tables. Then I saw this short little white French table at Heights Antiques on Yale. Originally it was probably a little telephone table or a nightstand. Although there were two, I just needed one. It was already painted, so I used it just the way it was.

Pair of Lamps

I knew the original lamps were too small, but I hadn't had time to replace them until now. If you look, you can see that they are tall and skinny. I didn't really have a specific lamp in mind for the bed, but I was trying to find one I liked that was less than $500 per lamp. I was delighted to find wood lamps with a linen shade. The height is nice, and the curves look French.

New Artwork above Bed

Because the bedding has changed, so too has the artwork. When I changed the bedding out, it was time to move

Purchase #4: New lamps

| 227 |

away from the yellow artwork in this room. It's not just about assembling things you love, but it's about selecting things that work together. I felt the artwork just wouldn't work with the new look. I wanted something that was more neutral for the wall above the bed. The room has nine-foot ceilings, and with a king-size bed, I felt it needed something *big*. I tried several looks, but in the end, I went with a French mirror and ironstone platters above the bed. The arrangement is large but is now the width of the bed. The mirror is French, while the ironstone is farmhouse. I love the simple color palette and how soothing it is.

New Artwork or Mirror above the Desk

I wasn't sure what I was going to put above the desk, I just knew the colors in the old painting weren't working with the blue and white. This is a problem that wasn't as obvious until I photo-graphed the room. The pair of bergère chairs and the bed looked like they belonged in a blue room, while the other side of the room (the desk and the linen press) looked like it belonged in a green and yellow room. I decided to move the large painting out and replace it with something else. As I was strolling through Chippendale Antiques in Houston, I found a lovely French mirror. The shop owner thought it was about a hundred years old. After inspecting it, I suspect she is right.

Before and after purchase #5:
Large French mirror and ironstone platters.

I like just having one chair here instead of three. Using all three chairs made the space look crowded. Switching to just one chair, changing out the busy artwork for one mirror, and simplifying what was on the desk made for a cleaner, simpler look.

Before and after purchase #6:
Neutral mirror

New Desk Chair

There wasn't anything wrong with the old chairs, I just wanted to add lots of French goodness to the room, so I wanted a French chair. I had an extra French chair sitting around (imagine that) so I moved it into the space. It's an antique, I suspect, from the 1800s. It has a bit of damage but nothing that would keep me from using it. I've had this chair for about twenty years, so it has been used in a variety of rooms. Because I really love the chair and it is small, I have been able to use it again and again. Sometimes we buy something we aren't crazy about just because we need a particular piece of furniture right away or because it is the right price. That's the type of furniture we end up not keeping. Try to buy only things you love. When you see something that makes your heart sing, buy it. When you dearly love the piece of furniture, you will find a way to keep it even if you have to move it occasionally from one room to another.

Blue Accents

I was loving the changes, but the room still needed something. I liked the pale, neutral palette, but a room needs some color to pop. I added blue pillows with sweet little mother-of-pearl buttons to the bergère chairs. I found pillows that more closely matched the duvet in color, but I didn't like those. Don't buy something just because it is the right color. You won't like it down the road. The pillows' small size worked well with the petite chairs. I tried a few different pillow combinations on the bed. The basket of magazines got moved from the sitting area to the desk. The magazines add a bit of color to the room. Notice I used magazines with blue and white on the covers for the container.

I used fresh flowers to add color and happiness to the room. The blue throw in the basket at the end of the bed repeats the blue as well.

Before and after with new basket and white basin.

Linen Press

I wasn't unhappy with the styling of the linen press. I just thought I would make a small change. I get tired of a look after a while, so it's nice to move things around. I didn't buy anything new; I just pulled things from other places. The added basket and enamel bowl are both vintage.

Before and After Lavender Girls' Bedroom

The girls' room at the farm had a touch of French flair. The beds, if not French, were certainly French-ish. (I define *French-ish* as maybe not French but something that is curvy, delicate, and feminine.) The beds are definitely French-ish.

From my initial assessment, I was unhappy with the red rug. Although I did pick out the rug, and I love flat weave rugs, I decided the rug wasn't going to work with the new direction I was taking the room. I wanted the room to look a bit more French and not quite so red. So I wanted to get rid of the red dresser and the red rug. I also wanted to move the farm chair out of the room. And I just didn't like the lamps on the dresser anymore. I originally bought them to go in the blue room shown previously in green, because they were green and went with that color pallet. When I changed colors, I didn't like the lamps, so they went. Had I adored the lamps, I would have found a place for them somewhere. This is an example of what I have been saying. I bought them because they were the right color, not because I liked them. So when I changed colors, I got rid of the lamps. The antique French nightstands were, of course, staying.

Before Photos

BEFORE AND AFTER

1. I removed the dresser because it was too red and it didn't work in the direction I was going.

2. The chair was removed because it was not French, and it was pretty wobbly.

3. I wanted to get rid of the rug because it was too red and it was not in keeping with my new vision.

4. I didn't like the dresser lamps anymore. I wasn't even that crazy about them when I bought them. Lesson learned.

5. The mirror was also going. I liked it but didn't think it would go with a new French dresser.

To give a room French accents, you do *not* need to get rid of everything that isn't French. I was tired of many things in this room, so this was a good time to replace them.

Beds

The beds felt too bland all white, so I decided I would add a little bit of color to the beds. I didn't want too much color, just a hint. To be completely transparent, I didn't know what I would like, so I tried a few different options. Some people said that this room without color looked like a hospital ward at Downton Abbey. I doubt that was meant as a compliment, but I thought that was pretty funny and true.

Here I tried a few different looks. First I added red and white duvets. I tried them spread out over the length of the bed and folded at the foot of the bed. Then I used the oversized throws, which were lovely. I want you to see that I tried several different options. In the end, I found some lavender gingham duvets that worked perfectly. I kept the throws for use elsewhere.

Chest

The old chest had color that was too strong. I also wanted an antique with graceful lines. The new chest, which isn't new at all, looks like it was made for the room. I found it at Heights Antiques on Yale. It was a beautiful chest with lots of details.

Lamp

I never did like the old lamps. The new lamp was simply moved in from the master bedroom. I gave the white set of lamps away to someone who was happy to have them. I bought the new lamp secondhand. It was brass and had a dated shade at the time. I replaced the shade with a new linen drum-shaped one. I painted the brass lamp base with black paint to give it an updated look.

Mirror

The old mirror didn't look right with the French chest, so as soon as I found the chest, I knew the mirror would have to be sold or given away. The new French mirror also adds presence to the room. It's tall and has a soft green color.

Rugs

I took out the large red rug. I still like it, just not in here. Rather than replace it with another large, expensive wool rug, I found some small ones to go between the beds. They were much cheaper, and I didn't really need one big rug in here.

Before and after with the stained chest and the soft French green mirror.

Before and after with the brass lamp painted black.

Make Mistakes

One reason I wanted to include the process I used on these rooms is because I think sometimes people believe, incorrectly, that designers and decorators have some magic touch, and that they get it right all the time with no mistakes and no experimenting. That is simply not true. If this mythological person exists, I would love to meet him or her. Decorating is trial and error, one step forward and two steps back—especially in the beginning. It's okay to make mistakes. That is part of the process. The point is to learn from your mistakes and not hit yourself over the head. With each mistake, you are learning. Everyone has to start out as a beginner. To be a good decorator, you have to be willing to be a bad one first.

If something doesn't work, try something else. Try to figure out what about the room isn't working. That will help you determine what you should do to fix it. If you don't know which pillow is the best one for your room, buy five and try them all. Keep the one that works and return the rest. The more you focus on your decorating skills, the more you will improve.

If you are stumped, ask for help. You can ask a friend who has a good eye or hire a professional. Some stores will even help you for free. Read books on design, subscribe to design blogs, and look at magazines. There are so many resources available. Save ideas on Pinterest.com or Houzz.com. Also, don't forget to photograph your room. Looking at those photos will be an invaluable exercise, even if you are the only one looking at them. Those photos will tell you what is working and not working.

So how did I know this would all work together? Well, clearly I didn't, because I had to make a few adjustments to my original plan.

After I finish a room, I ask myself if it holds together. Does it look better than it did before? Does it excite me now, or does it feel ho-hum? I usually know when I see the photos if I am done or not. Of course, even when I am done, I'm never really "done."

Before and after with the red rug switched out for neutral ones.

CHAPTER 19: PUTTING IT ALL TOGETHER

Decorating is a process. Don't feel bad if you buy something and it doesn't work. This happens to talented designers and decorators all the time. Sometimes you have a plan in your head, but it looks different when you put it all together. You will need to make some adjustments as you go. Even after I decorate a room, it often still needs something else. Sometimes a rug needs to be exchanged or something I ordered isn't the color I expected it to be. After I make all of the planned changes to a room, I step back and take a second look. I look at all of the changes along with what was already in the room. Does it all work together? Is it pleasing to the eye? Rarely does a plan come together without some tweaking. Let's say you did your analysis of the room, photographed it, put together a shopping list, and followed your plan to a T, and it still looks not quite right. Don't panic. Just step back and try to determine what isn't working. Take another photo and look at it again. Phone a friend. If you have a friend with a good eye, ask him or her what you should do. At the end of the day, it is your house, and you need to love the way it looks. All is not lost if you aren't happy with the room. It might only need some slight tweaking.

What Should You Do If Your Room Still Isn't Right?

Let's try our original exercise and see if we can get your room just the way you want it. This is meant to be a tool to help you put a plan together for your house.

Go outside and come in your home with fresh eyes. Pretend you are a visitor in your home. You can even bring a friend with you who will be honest with you. Walk into the room and pretend like you have never seen it before.

1. What is the first thing you notice about the room?

2. What feeling does it evoke?

3. Does it feel warm and inviting?

4. Is this a room you enjoy being in?

5. Does it feel dated?

6. What do you like about the room?

7. What would you like to change about the room?

8. Do you like the colors in the room?

9. Does the room feel cluttered?

10. Does the room flow, or does it feel choppy?

11. Does it feel balanced?

12. Do the colors and patterns work together or feel like they are fighting?

13. Is the furniture functional for the room?

With the answers from this list, begin to tweak the room. Take some photos and examine them. I am hopeful your home is getting closer to where you want it to be. It may take a while for you to get the room just like you want it. I have been tweaking my house for years. It's okay to try different things and move things around. Buy some new things, but keep the tags in case you want to return them. If you are still stuck, then seek some professional decorating advice. Even if you just hire someone for a two-hour consultation, that will be well worth the money spent. An expert can often tell you things that might take you years to figure out on your own. We all get stuck in a rut, thinking things have to be arranged the way they are. New eyes, especially when they belong to someone talented, can provide some wonderful, fresh ideas.

If you use a professional, be sure to show them your notes for the assessment above. Write down any specific questions you have for your decorator. Make good use of your time. Listen and try not to talk too much. You are usually paying per hour. Some decorators will even work with you online using your photos. They don't always need to come to your home.

PUTTING IT ALL TOGETHER

So what if you realize now that you have made some decorating mistakes? Breathe! It's not the end of the world. I make mistakes all the time. This is how we learn and grow. My motto is, if you aren't making mistakes, then you aren't learning anything. If you purchased something you dislike, hopefully it is returnable. If it isn't and you just can't stand it, then think about consigning it to a consignment store or selling it on Craigslist or eBay. If you don't like a paint color you used on a chair, maybe you can paint it again in another color. It is helpful if you can limit your mistakes to small-ticket items. Ovens and refrigerators are difficult to return and expensive to replace.

Let's say you bought something you don't like and you don't have a place you can sell it. Do you have a friend who likes it? If so, can you do an exchange? There is usually a way to fix most anything. Sometimes you just need to be a bit creative. When I make a mistake, I try to figure out a way to fix it. Sometimes the fix is easy if it just requires a return. One time, I started painting a wall. I hated the color. I wondered if I should stop. Then I looked at how many gallons of paint I just bought. I kept painting. I wondered if maybe it would look better when I finished the wall. It didn't. Then I thought maybe it would look better once the paint dried. It didn't. Note: As soon as you notice you don't like a shade of paint, STOP. Don't keep painting, thinking you will like it better later. I don't care how many gallons of paint you bought.
Trust me—you will be sorry.

Sometimes I buy a chair and I don't end up liking it in the room I bought it for, but it works great in another one. Things get rotated a lot at our house. That's another reason to keep similar colors in several rooms, so you can move things around if you want to.

Decorating a home is not something you do just once. Your home should evolve with you as your tastes change and grow. It's okay to mix things up and change your home. Experiment and have fun.

CHAPTER 20: FINAL THOUGHTS

I'm going over all that I covered and thinking, did I forget something? Did I leave something out? What do I really want you to remember? I know this is the last chapter, and this is my last chance to reveal decorating ideas. What are the things I really want you to remember?

Create Your Own Style—Don't Just Follow the Fads

Your home should showcase your style, not the latest fad. Your home needs to embrace you, your family, and your friends. In my mind, it's not about showing off. It's about making your home special for you. I know some people make decorating a competitive sport, but please don't get caught up in that. It can be expensive in more ways than one. The competitiveness can make decorating stressful. If you are just redoing your home to impress others, then you may feel the need to change things out unnecessarily every year or two. If you select furniture that will impress but is not necessarily what you like, then you aren't going to be happy with it, and you will end up replacing it or detesting it. Decorating should be fun, not stressful. I don't suggest going with every fad, but it is wise to keep up with trends, meaning you should at least know what they are. You want to know what is in and what is out. Then keep that in mind when purchasing new things—especially big purchases. For example, you wouldn't want to buy a blue stove if they were on their way out unless you really, really, really like blue stoves. That would be expensive to replace. But a blue pillow is typically not a big expense and could easily be replaced later when you tire of blue or it goes out of style.

Pace Yourself

Try to find things for your home that you love, but you don't have to buy it all in one day or even one month. I would rather have two things I am crazy about than fifty ho-hum things. It's okay if it takes time to create the home you love. It probably will. The trap too many people fall into is buying something they can afford but don't like. Remember, if you don't like it, I don't care what

a great deal you got it for, you paid too much. Learn to embrace those empty spaces while you wait for that perfect something.

Step Out of Your Comfort Zone

I hope this book has encouraged you to try some new things, and maybe step out of your comfort zone. To get a unique, beautiful look requires thoughtful reflection. I believe our homes affect our mood to a large degree. A beautiful, peaceful home is so important, especially as the world becomes a crazier place every day. Trust your instincts. Your style won't be the same as mine or anyone else's. You have your own unique look. Even if your look is still evolving, it is your look, and you have the final say on what works and what doesn't in your home.

Sometimes clients have a piece I really don't like. I ask if they are open to moving or getting rid of it. If they say they want to keep it, I honor that, because it is their house, not mine. Sometimes I do things in my home and readers hate it. I usually consider their argument. Sometimes I end up agreeing, and I make the change they recommend. However, sometimes I just flat disagree. If I don't agree, then I do it the way I want to without apology. I have to live in this house. The homeowner gets the final say. If a designer tries to bring a piece in that you don't like, speak up.

Don't Assume Your Family Doesn't Care

I have a story to share with you. My daughter has never had any interest in interior design; she loves music. That's fine with me. I want her to be who she is. I accepted the fact a long time ago that she probably won't notice my decorating skills. Then one day I asked her if she wanted some crystal lamps in her room. She was so excited and told me that they would make her room feel like paradise. It was a nice and unexpected compliment. That goes to show that even if your family doesn't compliment you on your decorating abilities, they probably still appreciate them.

Understand Decorating Is a Journey

Another thing I want to tell you is that it takes time for your style to evolve and emerge. Don't expect to knock it out of the ballpark your first time at bat. My first attempts at decorating were pretty embarrassing. Here's the thing about learning something new. You have to be willing to be bad at it in the beginning. Even if your first attempts aren't that great, don't give up. Failure is part of the learning process. Any forward movement is progress.

The Importance of Decorating

Some people see interior decorating as unimportant, but I don't agree. Our homes are where we live out most of our lives. They will have an impact on the quality of our lives. The impact can be positive or negative. We entertain our friends and spend time with family in our homes. I want those people to feel welcome and loved. I hope that my home helps them to feel special. A decorated home is all about how it makes people feel when they are there. It's not about having the nicest house on the block or impressing visitors with how much money you have. I want those visitors to feel inspired to create their own beautiful spaces. I want to create a welcoming environment where guests and family feel celebrated. If we can do that, then we have done something important.

FURNITURE & DECOR SOURCES

ABOUT THE AUTHOR

When asked what she wanted to be when she grew up, Anita Joyce would always answer "an artist," until her father convinced her she would be poor for the rest of her life. Fearing that she would live in a van down by the river, she turned her attention to engineering and a respectable life in the suburbs. During the day, she wore steel-toed shoes and a hard hat to work, while in the evenings she made her own curtains and slipcovers. This was the secret she hid from her male coworkers.

Working as an engineer, then as a corporate quality consultant, she had an expense account and a closet full of suits. She enjoyed her work, but she wondered if there was something more. Later, her first child, a daughter, was born with Down syndrome. Due to her daughter's health issues, Anita left the corporate world to become a full-time mom. Soon a second daughter arrived. Anita began to look for creative outlets and opened a photography business. Later she worked for a furniture store and began to soak up every bit of knowledge she could about interior decorating and design. As her kids got older, her family left the suburbs for an historic neighborhood in the heart of the city.

In 2011, she took the plunge and hit *publish* for the first time on her blog (www.cedarhillfarmhouse.com). The *Cedar Hill Farmhouse* blog, named for the family's Round Top farm, is a way for Anita to encourage readers in their decorating pursuits. The blog opened up a new world to her. She connected with thousands of like-minded people around the globe. They understood her need to create a beautiful home, because they too felt the same way. Her work has appeared in many national print magazines, including *Flea Market Décor* and *Romantic Homes*. She has been featured on many websites, including Apartment Therapy, Houzz.com, and the Better Homes and Gardens website. She has curated collections for Joss and Main, and she currently writes for Houzz.com. In 2014 she won the Best of Houzz award. Previously, she served as a mentor at the Thrive Blog Conference and as a contributor to the *Celebrating Everyday Life* magazine.

Anita, her husband, their two girls, and their collie, Molly, divide their time between Houston and Round Top, Texas.